Cover illustration: *The Crucifixion* by Gustave Doré
Colorized and modified by William Britton

D1303615

Table of Contents

List of Illustrations

List of Maps

List of Figures

1

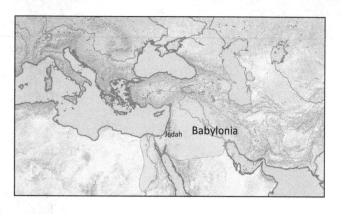

BABYLONIA (626-539 B.C.)

- Head of gold in Daniel's statue
- Destroyed Jerusalem and the temple and carried Judah into captivity in 586 B.C.

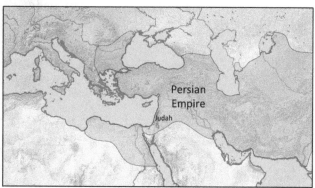

PERSIAN EMPIRE (539-332 BC)

- Chest and arms of silver in Daniel's statue
- Darius captured Babylon in 539 B.C.

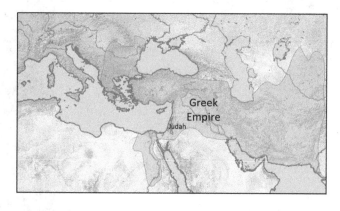

GREEK EMPIRE (332-63 BC)

- Belly and thighs of bronze in Daniel's statue
- Alexander the Great defeated the Persians in 332 B.C.

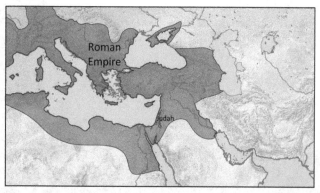

ROMAN EMPIRE (63 BC- 476 AD)

- Legs of iron and feet of iron and clay in Daniel's statue
- Roman General Pompey conquered Jerusalem in 63 B.C.

The Times of the Gentiles (Intertestamental Period)

OVERVIEW

Israel returned to the land and rebuilt the temple and the walls of Jerusalem 70 years after their captivity—as God had promised. Upon their return, however, they found a sort of new world order. Israel had been an independent nation called to shine their light out to other nations. Now, they were under the control of Gentile kingdoms and were to shine their light from within. Instead of faithfully shining that light, however, the people fell into two different traps. Some clothed themselves with the culture and customs of their Gentile lords such that they were indistinguishable from those whom they were called to reach. Others separated themselves so that the Gentiles *could not* be invited into a relationship with God. During this time, God was preparing the world for Jesus who would show Israel a new way of shining the light, a way that was faithful to the Old Testament Law and faithful to shine the light to the nations.

SOURCE MATERIAL

- Daniel 2:31-45, 11:1-39
- Psalm 137
- *Rose Book of Bible Charts, Maps and Timelines*, pages 68-72
- *The Four* by Peter Leithart, Chapter 1 (for further study)

ACTIVITIES

1. Daniel's Statue. Read Daniel 2:31-35 and, on the following page, draw the statue that Nebuchadnezzar saw in his dream. Label each section of the statue with the appropriate kingdom. Use your creativity in your drawing.

Daniel's Statue (cont.)

2. Separation and Accommodation. During the time between the Old Testament and the New Testament, the Jewish people were exiled among foreign nations, and then later, lived in Israel under the rule of the Greeks and Romans. During this time, many Jews became just like the Greeks (accommodation). On the other hand, Jews who didn't want to become like the Greeks tended to completely separate themselves from Greek culture, creating their own isolated communities (separation). In both of these ways of relating to the world (accommodation and separation) they failed to properly shine the light into the Gentile world. The same temptations are present in the lives of all Christians today. Fill in the blanks in the following chart with how a Christian who is trying to separate from the world might behave in each of these areas of life. Do the same for the Christian who is trying to accommodate the world in each of these areas. Finally, fill in the blank for how a Christian should behave to shine the light without accommodating in each of these areas of life. The, answer the questions on the following page.

Area of Life	Separation	Accommodation	Shine The Light
Music, movies, tv			
Relationships with unbelievers			
Sports			
Politics			

Which temptation are you more attracted to: accommodation or separation? _____

_____

_____

_____

What can you do to help protect yourself from that temptation?_____

_____

_____

_____

_____

_____

_____

_____

_____

_____

EVALUATION

1. What do each of the different sections of the statue in Daniel 2 represent? _____

_____

_____

2. What does the rock not cut with hands represent out of Daniel 2? _____

_____

3. Who were the Maccabees? _____

_____

_____

4. Who were the Hasmoneans and how were they connected with the Maccabees? _____

_____

_____

5. Who was Herod the Great, and in what way did he set the stage for the coming of the Messiah? ____

_____

_____

_____

6. How did the world and Israel's relationship with it change after the return from exile? _____

_____

_____

_____

7. How did Israel do at shining their light from within? _____

_____

_____

In what ways did they fail? _____

_____

_____

The New Creation

OVERVIEW

The incarnation of Jesus Christ changes *everything*. The incarnation changes the way believers read Genesis 1 and therefore, the entire Old Testament. Furthermore, the incarnation transforms the old creation to a new creation from the inside out.

SOURCE MATERIAL

- John 1:1-3, 14, 16-18
- Genesis 1:1-5
- 2 Corinthians 5:17
- Psalm 149
- *Rose Book of Bible Charts, Maps and Timelines*, pages 180-183

ACTIVITIES

1. Trinity Analogy Project. There are a number of common analogies that are used to try to explain how there can be only one God, yet three persons in the Trinity. All of these analogies ultimately fail and actually teach a false view of the Trinity. For each of the following analogies, write an explanation of what is wrong with the analogy in the space below it. Finally, invent your own analogy for the Trinity and explain where it goes wrong in explaining the Trinity.

False Analogy #1: God is like an egg. There is only one egg, but three parts: the shell, yolk and white. Likewise, God is made up of the Father, Son and Holy Spirit. What is wrong with this analogy?_____

_____

_____

_____

_____

_____

False Analogy #2: God is like water that exists in three different forms: solid (ice), liquid (water) and gas (water vapor). Likewise, God appears as three forms: Father, Son and Holy Spirit. What is wrong with this analogy?_____

_____

_____

_____

Write your own analogy:_____

_____

_____

_____

What is wrong with your own analogy?_____

_____

_____

2. Journal Time: Transformation. The incarnation of Jesus Christ changes the old creation into an entirely new creation, from the inside out. The incarnation means that transformation for sinners is possible. Spend some time writing in your journal or the space below. Identify an area in your life where you need transformation and write out a prayer, asking God to transform even those areas you have the hardest time believing will ever change._____

_____

_____

_____

_____

3. Psalm Singing Activity. Sing or read Psalm 149 and write a short prayer of thanksgiving to God in the space below._____

_____

_____

_____

_____

EVALUATION

1. What does John 1:1-3 tell us about Genesis 1:1-3? _____

_____

_____

_____

2. What does the fact that the Son was with God in the beginning tell us about the rest of the Old Testament? _____

_____

_____

_____

3. How does the incarnation impact all of creation? _____

_____

_____

_____

4. What does the incarnation mean for us as Christians?_____

_____

_____

_____

OVERVIEW

Jesus is the culmination of the seed-line: the line of descendants promised to ultimately produce *a* Seed who would crush the head of the serpent. Jesus is the new Adam, the Son of Abraham and the promised Son of David. The hope that humanity will be redeemed from the fall rests on this promised Son for whom Israel had been waiting for many generations. Matthew and Luke both record a genealogy of Jesus Christ to prove that He had the proper lineage to be the Messiah.

SOURCE MATERIAL

- Matthew 1:1-17
- Luke 3:23-38
- Genesis 3:15
- Psalm 89
- *Rose Book of Bible Charts, Maps and Timelines*, page 80

ACTIVITIES

1. Construct the Genealogy. Matthew and Luke both record genealogies for Jesus. The genealogy according to Matthew is written on the following page. Break the genealogy up according to the following passages, labeling each section with the appropriate passage where the genealogical record is recorded in the Old Testament. After Zerubbabel, the names were taken from Joseph's family records and are not recorded in the Old Testament. Use the following Old Testament passages for this assignment: Genesis 25:19, 26, 35:22-26, 38:29; Ruth 4:18-22; 1 Chronicles 3:1-17.

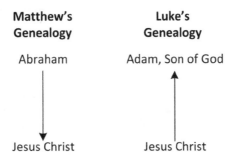

Matthew's Genealogy	Luke's Genealogy
Abraham	Adam, Son of God
↓	↑
Jesus Christ	Jesus Christ

Abraham	Obed	Ahaz	Zadok
Isaac	Jesse	Hezekiah	Achim
Jacob	David & wife of Uriah	Manasseh	Eliud
Judah & Tamar	Solomon	Amon	Eleazar
Perez	Rehoboam	Josiah	Matthan
Hezron	Abijam	Jeconiah	Jacob
Ram	Asa	Shealtiel	Joseph & Mary
Amminadab	Jehoshaphat	Zerubbabel	Jesus
Nahshon	Jehoram	Abiud	
Salmon & Rahab	Uzziah	Eliakim	
Boaz & Ruth	Jotham	Azor	

2. My Family Tree. Our culture doesn't value genealogies as much as Jesus' culture did or even other modern-day cultures do. A genealogy or family tree and the family history that accompanies it can provide a source of identity; when we know our family history, we know that we belong within a greater story. Make a family tree going back three generations (to your great-grandparents). In addition to finding names of people, try to find stories of your ancestors. (As with any family, your family is made of human sinners, so not all of the stories you discover will be good ones. Your teacher will help you pray through any difficult stories you find in your family's history.)

_____
(me)

_____   _____
(my dad)   (my mom)

_____   _____   _____   _____
(dad's dad)   (dad's mom)   (mom's dad)   (mom's mom)

_____   _____   _____   _____   _____   _____   _____   _____
(great   (great   (great   (great   (great   (great   (great   (great
grandpa) grandma) grandpa) grandma) grandpa) grandma) grandpa) grandma)

After making your family tree, write out one of your favorite stories and what it means to you, in the space below._____

_____

_____

_____

_____

_____

_____

_____

_____

_____

_____

EVALUATION

1. What are the main differences between Luke's and Matthew's genealogies? _____

_____

_____

2. Why does Luke's genealogy end at Adam? _____

_____

3. Why does Matthew's start at Abraham? _____

_____

4. Why is it important to have a record of Jesus' ancestry?_____

_____

_____

Miraculous Births: John and Jesus

OVERVIEW

Much like the period of the Judges when Israel was oppressed by the Philistines and a host of Canaanites, during the time of Jesus' birth, Israel was under the oppression of a variety of evil forces (demons, disease, wicked religious leaders and Roman overlords). During the period of the Judges, God caused not just one, but two miraculous births to bring about the deliverance of His people: Samson and Samuel were both born to barren women at the same time. Now again, God used two miraculous births to deliver His people. Both births were announced by angels, and while Mary received the news with faith, Zechariah did not.

SOURCE MATERIAL

- **Luke 1:1-2:40**
- Matthew 1:18-2:12
- 1 Samuel 1:1-2:11
- Judges 13:1-25

ACTIVITIES

1. Faith and Joy, Doubt and Bitterness. In order to understand the connections between faith and joy and between doubt and bitterness, answer the following questions, based on Luke 1:1-2:40. Be prepared to discuss your answers.

What happened to Zechariah as a result of his doubt? _____

_____

_____

What do you think it was like for Zechariah to be unable to speak? _____

_____

_____

_____

_____

What was Mary able to do right away because of her faith? _____

_____

_____

This story teaches us that faith in God's promises leads to rejoicing, but doubt leads to an inability to praise God. When we doubt Him, God doesn't usually take away our ability to speak. Instead, doubt leads to something worse than silence—the ability to make noise but not rejoice. What are some examples of this type of noise? _____

_____

_____

_____

_____

What's an example of a time in your life when you have noticed either how faith has led to joy or how doubt has led to a lack of joy? _____

_____

_____

_____

_____

_____

_____

2. Sing the Magnificat. One of the best ways to enter into the biblical narrative is to sing the songs that they were singing. Search on YouTube for "Keith and Kristen Getty - Magnificat" and sing along with it. Put yourself in Mary or Joseph's shoes while you sing. Write a short paragraph below with your reaction._____

_____

_____

_____

_____

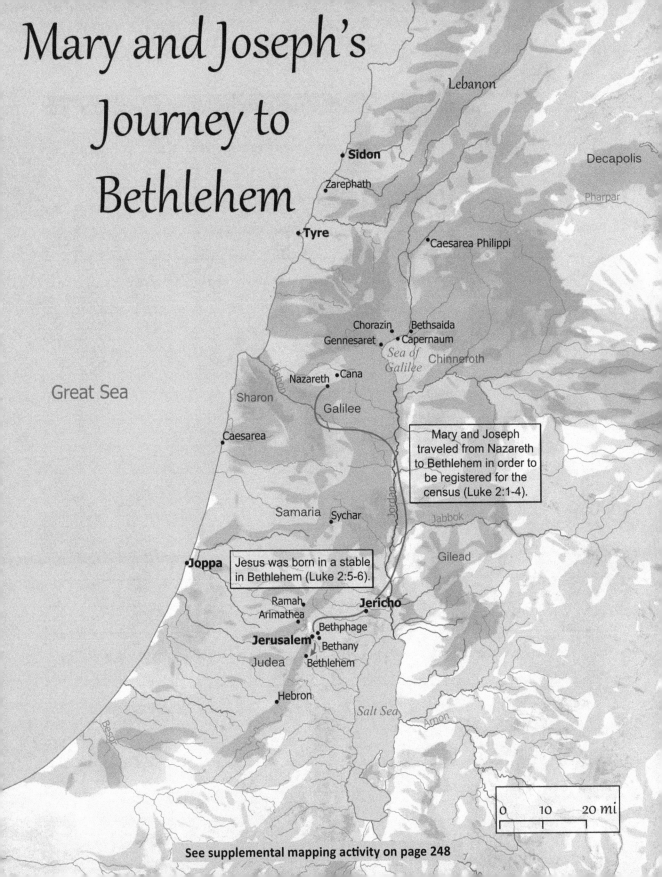

Mary and Joseph's Journey to Bethlehem

Lebanon

•**Sidon**

Zarephath•

Decapolis

Pharpar

•**Tyre**

•Caesarea Philippi

Chorazin• •Bethsaida
Gennesaret• •Capernaum

Sea of Galilee Chinneroth

Nazareth• •Cana

Sharon

Galilee

Great Sea

Caesarea•

Mary and Joseph
traveled from Nazareth
to Bethlehem in order to
be registered for the
census (Luke 2:1-4).

Samaria• •Sychar

Jabbok

Gilead

•**Joppa**

Jesus was born in a stable
in Bethlehem (Luke 2:5-6).

Ramah•
Arimathea•

•**Jericho**

Bethphage•
Jerusalem• •Bethany

Judea •Bethlehem

Hebron•

Salt Sea

Arnon

Besor

0   10   20 mi

See supplemental mapping activity on page 248

EVALUATION

1. What is the Old Testament significance of a barren woman getting pregnant? _____

_____

2. What is the significance of both a virgin and a barren woman bearing a son? _____

_____

_____

3. What is the significance of two miraculous conceptions at about the same time?_____

_____

4. What do Samson and John the Baptist have in common?_____

_____

_____

_____

5. What do Jesus and Samuel have in common? _____

_____

_____

_____

6. Why did Elizabeth call Mary "Most blessed among women" (Luke 1:42)? _____

_____

_____

_____

7. What were the different responses to the angelic announcement for Zechariah and Mary? _____

_____

_____

8. What did Zechariah's doubt cost him? _____

_____

_____

Jesus' Flight to Egypt: Jesus is the New Israel

OVERVIEW

Herod had heard from the Magi that there was a king born in Bethlehem. He was hoping to find out from the Magi who this king was so he could kill Him to secure his throne. The Magi, however, outwitted him and returned to their land by a different route. Herod became angry and gave orders to kill all the boys two years of age and under. An angel warned Joseph, so Jesus' family fled to Egypt where they remained until Herod died. Joseph and his family then returned to Israel and raised Jesus in Nazareth. Throughout this lesson, we see parallels between Jesus and the period of Israel's exodus; Jesus is the new Israel.

SOURCE MATERIAL

- Matthew 2:1-23
- Exodus 1

ACTIVITIES

1. Count the Cost. Calculate how much the gifts of gold, frankincense and myrrh were worth in the first century, but calculated in today's dollars. We don't know exactly how much the magi brought to Jesus, but just assume a fairly small amount of each, perhaps 1 pound. Use Internet sources to try to calculate the cost as best you can.

Value of one pound of gold in the first century (in today's dollars): $_____

Value of one pound of frankincense in the first century (in today's dollars): $_____

Value of one pound of myrrh in the first century (in today's dollars): $_____

Total Value: $_____

2. Journal Time: The Magi's Sacrifice. Spend some time thinking about all the sacrifices the Magi made in order to come worship a child. They traveled a very long distance, gave him very expensive gifts, and provoked the wrath of King Herod by not obeying his command to tell him who the child was. They risked so much, just so they could worship Jesus, because they knew what the arrival of this child meant for them. They showed profound faith, incredible generosity and a deeply burning desire to worship the Lord. Reflect on your own life, then write about the following in your journal or the space below.

Do you desire to worship the Lord anywhere near as much as the Magi did?_____

_____

_____

_____

_____

What sacrifices have you had to make or have been unwilling to make in order to worship the Lord?___

_____

_____

_____

_____

The Magi were willing to sacrifice their time, money, comfort and safety in order to worship Jesus, because they understood how important He is. Pray that God would open your eyes to see what you are missing out on by not worshipping Jesus with your whole heart. Pray that your desire to worship the Lord would grow. Write a short prayer in the space below._____

_____

_____

_____

_____

_____

_____

_____

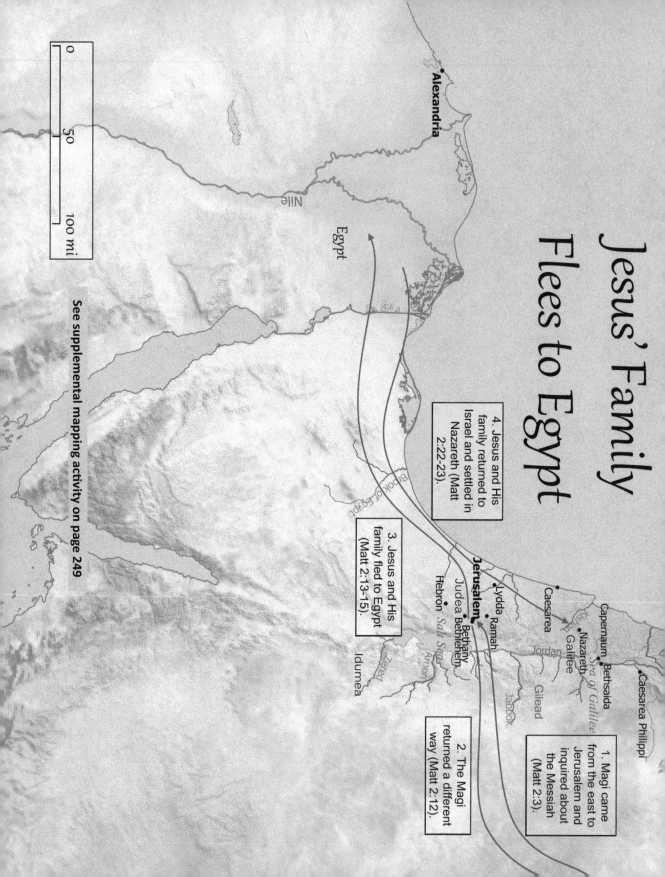

Jesus' Family
Flees to Egypt

0   50   100 mi

See supplemental mapping activity on page 249

Alexandria

Nile

Egypt

Brook of Egypt

Idumea

4. Jesus and His
family returned to
Israel and settled in
Nazareth (Matt
2:22-23).

3. Jesus and His
family fled to Egypt
(Matt 2:13-15).

Jerusalem

Hebron Bethlehem
Judea Bethany
Ramah
Lydda

Caesarea

Capernaum Bethsaida
Nazareth
Sea of Galilee
Galilee
Jordan
Gilead
Jabbok
Arnon
Salt Sea

Caesarea Philippi

1. Magi came
from the east to
Jerusalem and
inquired about
the Messiah
(Matt 2:3).

2. The Magi
returned a different
way (Matt 2:12).

EVALUATION

1. What is significant about the Magi coming from a foreign land?_____

_____

_____

2. Why was Herod so threatened by the baby King in Bethlehem? _____

_____

_____

_____

3. What Old Testament character was Herod similar to?_____

_____

_____

4. In what way is Jesus the new Israel? _____

_____

_____

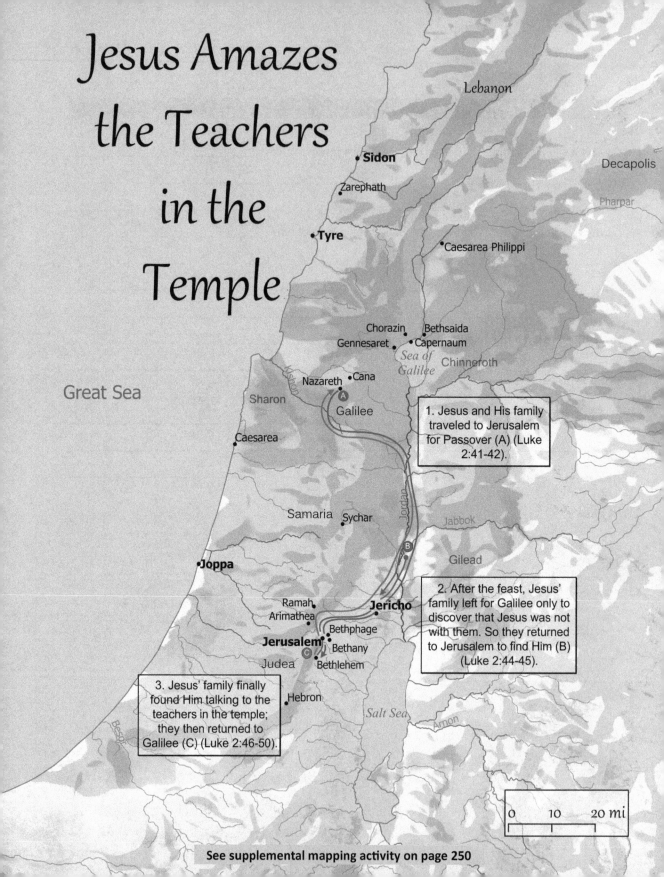

Jesus Amazes the Teachers in the Temple

Lebanon

Decapolis

Pharpar

Sidon

Zarephath

Tyre

Caesarea Philippi

Great Sea

Chorazin

Bethsaida

Gennesaret

Capernaum

Sea of Galilee

Chinneroth

Nazareth

Cana

Galilee

1. Jesus and His family traveled to Jerusalem for Passover (A) (Luke 2:41-42).

Sharon

Caesarea

Samaria

Sychar

Jordan

Jabbok

Gilead

Joppa

Ramah

Arimathea

Jericho

Bethphage

Jerusalem

Bethany

Judea

Bethlehem

Hebron

Salt Sea

Arnon

2. After the feast, Jesus' family left for Galilee only to discover that Jesus was not with them. So they returned to Jerusalem to find Him (B) (Luke 2:44-45).

3. Jesus' family finally found Him talking to the teachers in the temple; they then returned to Galilee (C) (Luke 2:46-50).

Besor

Kishon

0   10   20 mi

See supplemental mapping activity on page 250

The Foreshadowing of Jesus' Temple Ministry

OVERVIEW

Samuel was the prophet called to supplant the wicked priests, and Jesus is the new Samuel. Even as a 12-year-old, Jesus spent time in His true Father's house, questioning and answering the priests. This story foreshadows His later questioning of the priests in the temple. This questioning would ultimately lead to His arrest, death and resurrection upon which He would ascend to His Father's right hand and supplant the wicked priests.

SOURCE MATERIAL

- Luke 2:41-52
- 1 Samuel 1-2
- Proverbs 1:8

ACTIVITIES

1. Compare Jesus to Samuel. Read 1 Samuel 1-2 and Luke 2:41-52 and, on the next page, make a list of as many similarities between Samuel and Jesus as young men. Use your creativity; it doesn't have to be an exact similarity to make it onto the list, just find as many as you can.

Samuel	Jesus

2. Journal Time: 12-Year-Old Jesus. As a 12-year-old, Jesus was already becoming who He would be when He was grown up. Write in your journal or the space below, comparing yourself to Jesus at age 12. _____

_____

_____

_____

_____

_____

_____

_____

_____

_____

Read Luke 2:51-52. Jesus was perfect, yet even He was obedient to His imperfect parents. How much more so should you be obedient to your parents! How can you be more like Jesus by being more obedient to your parents?_____

_____

_____

_____

_____

_____

_____

_____

_____

_____

EVALUATION

1. In what ways was Jesus like Samuel?_____

_____

_____

_____

2. What did Jesus' interaction with the priests tell us about His later ministry in the temple?_____

_____

_____

_____

3. Why was Jesus surprised that His parents were shocked that He was in the temple? _____

_____

_____

_____

UNIT 2   **2**   JESUS' MINISTRY BEGINS

The Ministry of John the Baptist

OVERVIEW

While Jesus had come of age, John the Baptist had also come of age, and God led him out into the wilderness where he began to preach that the nation must prepare for the coming Messiah. By the way he conducted his ministry, John painted a picture: out of the corrupt establishment in Israel, God was calling a new people for Himself.

SOURCE MATERIAL

- **John 1:6-34**
- Matthew 3:1-11
- Mark 1:1-8
- Luke 3:1-19

ACTIVITIES

1. Being Bold. John the Baptist spoke boldly what God had called him to even though he was considered a nobody in Israel. Consider where God is calling you to be bold, to speak out about something. Maybe it's to oppose a bully; maybe it's to say "thank you" to someone (like a school janitor) who never gets thanked for his work. Maybe it's something else entirely. Brainstorm some things that God might be calling you to say and do that would require you to be a little uncomfortable; then, on the next page, write them in the column on the left. On the right side, across from each item on the left, write the reasons that you aren't currently doing these things. Put a star next to a couple of bold actions you want to do for God this week.

Bold things to do	Reasons why I'm not doing these things

2. John's Picture. When John was calling people to repent and be baptized, he was calling them to leave the bondage of Egypt (Israel) and be baptized in the Red Sea (baptism) so that God could make them into a new nation. God was calling out a new chosen people for Himself. Using the word bank below, fill in the blanks in the diagram, filling in the picture John was communicating. Each line in the diagram will have one term from the word bank.

WORD BANK:

Red Sea

New Nation

Leave Slavery

Baptism

Repent

Egypt

Israel

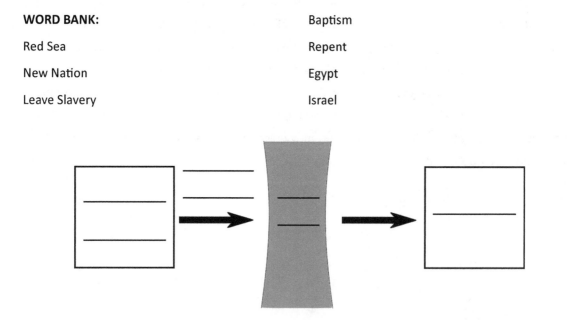

EVALUATION

1. In the eyes of the world, what were John's qualifications for the job God gave him? _____

_____

_____

2. What qualifications did God give John? Did He give John special education or a special title? _____

_____

_____

_____

3. What message did John preach? _____

_____

4. What picture did John's baptizing ministry present? _____

_____

_____

Jesus' Baptism

OVERVIEW

Jesus had returned from His exodus to Egypt, anticipated His ministry in the temple and grown up in His earthly father's house. Next, He met His forerunner John in the wilderness. Jesus underwent John's baptism, identifying with the new people John was calling out of Israel. Furthermore, Jesus' baptism continues the picture that Jesus is the new Israel and identifies Him as the new Joshua. God affirmed Jesus in His ministry by sending the Holy Spirit upon Him and speaking from heaven.

SOURCE MATERIAL

- **Matthew 3:13-16**
- Mark 1:9-11
- Luke 2:21-22
- John 1:29-34

ACTIVITIES

1. The Meaning of Water. Water is a part of our lives every day. But water is both a blessing and a source of hardship. The meaning of water in the Bible is built on the meaning of water in everyday life. Fill in the two lists below then answer the questions that follow.

Good things water does	Bad things water does

In general, is water a good thing, a bad thing, or both?_____

_____

_____

_____

What does the fact that something so necessary to life can also be the source of death teach you about God's world?_____

_____

_____

_____

Why do you think God chose baptism as the symbol of what it means to be a Christian in light of what you now know about water?_____

_____

_____

_____

2. Journal Time. Consider whether you are living as though you have already been accepted by God or if you are trying to work hard to earn God's acceptance. Answer the following questions in your journal or the space below (questions continued on the following page).

How do you picture God thinking about you—as a critical judge, inspecting your every move, waiting to point out and punish any wrong that you do, or as a loving Father, knowing all about you because He created you and loves you?_____

_____

_____

_____

When you do something "good," do you think that maybe you have earned God's acceptance or moved up a little higher on His "nice list"? Likewise, if you sin, do you feel that God no longer accepts you or that you are now on His "naughty list"?_____

_____

_____

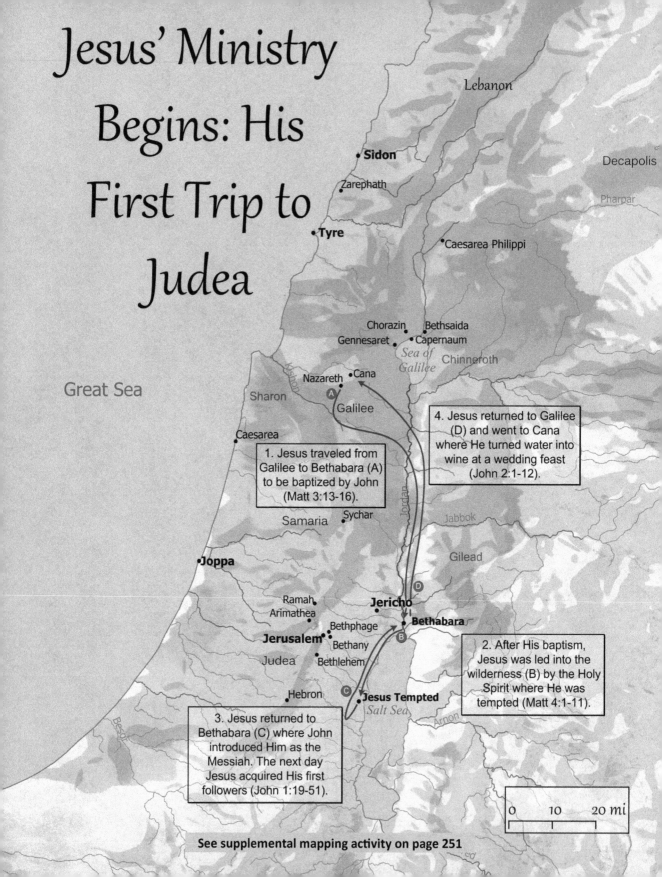

Jesus' Ministry Begins: His First Trip to Judea

1. Jesus traveled from Galilee to Bethabara (A) to be baptized by John (Matt 3:13-16).

2. After His baptism, Jesus was led into the wilderness (B) by the Holy Spirit where He was tempted (Matt 4:1-11).

3. Jesus returned to Bethabara (C) where John introduced Him as the Messiah. The next day Jesus acquired His first followers (John 1:19-51).

4. Jesus returned to Galilee (D) and went to Cana where He turned water into wine at a wedding feast (John 2:1-12).

See supplemental mapping activity on page 251

Lebanon

Decapolis

Pharpar

Sidon

Zarephath

Tyre

Caesarea Philippi

Chorazin Bethsaida

Gennesaret Capernaum

Sea of Galilee Chinneroth

Kishon

Nazareth Cana

(A)

Galilee

Great Sea

Sharon

Caesarea

Jordan

Jabbok

Samaria Sychar

Gilead

Joppa

(D)

Ramah

Arimathea Jericho

Bethphage Bethabara

Jerusalem (B)

Bethany

Judea Bethlehem

Hebron (C)

Jesus Tempted

Salt Sea

Arnon

Besor

0   10   20 mi

Think about your relationship with your earthly parents and how your relationship with your dad and mom affects your view of God._____

_____

_____

_____

EVALUATION

1. What does Jesus' baptism tell us?_____

_____

_____

_____

2. What does God's response to His baptism tell us about Jesus? _____

_____

_____

_____

Jesus' Fasting and Temptation

OVERVIEW

Immediately after His baptism, the Spirit took Jesus into the wilderness, where He fasted and was tempted as Adam and Eve were once tempted. Unlike them, He passed the test with flying colors.

SOURCE MATERIAL

- **Luke 4:1-13**
- Matthew 4:1-11
- Mark 1:12-23
- Genesis 3:1-7
- 1 John 2:15-17

ACTIVITIES

1. Understanding the Nature of Temptation. Read Genesis 3:1-7, Matthew 4:1-11, and 1 John 2:15-17. Use the table below to compare and contrast the temptations in these passages.

Genesis 3:1-17	Matthew 4:1-11	1 John 2:15-17

2. Journal Time: Dealing with Temptation. In your journal or the space below answer the following questions regarding temptation.

What is a temptation in your own life that seems to beat you regularly?_____

_____

_____

_____

What were Jesus' three temptations?_____

_____

_____

_____

Which of Jesus' three temptations is your temptation like?_____

_____

_____

_____

What might it look like to resist your temptation in a way Jesus would?_____

_____

_____

_____

Jesus' 40 days in the desert being tempted by the devil were the launchpad for three years of incredible ministry, all culminating in the crucifixion, resurrection, and ascension. What new things might open up for you, once you have beaten your temptation? Spend some time praying and thinking about this before you answer. _____

_____

_____

_____

_____

_____

EVALUATION

1. What were Jesus' three temptations? _____

_____

_____

_____

_____

2. Why would these three things have been wrong? _____

_____

_____

_____

_____

_____

_____

_____

3. How did Jesus resist each of the temptations? _____

_____

_____

_____

_____

_____

_____

_____

_____

John Passed the Baton to Jesus

OVERVIEW

John's ministry began before Jesus' did, and a great number of people came to repent and be baptized by him. But he was always looking forward to Jesus. When Jesus arrived, John humbly submitted to God's calling and became less as Christ became greater. Ultimately, John was imprisoned for his boldness and died at the hands of Herod; but he will always be remembered for making much of Jesus.

SOURCE MATERIAL

- **John 1:35-51, John 3:22-36**
- **Matthew 11:1-4**, 5-19
- **Mark** 1:4-8, 14-15, **6:14-29**
- **Luke** 3:15-18, **19-20**

ACTIVITIES

1. Timeline. Using John 1-3 and Mark 1:1-14 construct a rough timeline of the events of John and Jesus' ministries on the line on the following page. Actual times between events are often unknown, but include them where they are given. Make sure to include all the following events, but you can include more if you want.

The following events should be included on your timeline (given in no particular order):

- Jesus' ministry began.
- John began preaching in the wilderness.
- John was beheaded.
- Jesus went to Galilee for the wedding at Cana.
- John was imprisoned.
- John pointed to announce the Lamb of God.
- John baptized Jesus.
- Jesus went to Galilee.
- John pointed his disciples toward Jesus.

Timeline (cont.)

_____

2. Journal Time: Your Calling. John the Baptist was created by God to be this wild wilderness man who was to make a big deal of Jesus and then fade into the background. He was most fulfilled as a person when he followed this calling. Write in your journal or the space below, answering the following questions.

What is something you feel most fulfilled doing?_____

_____

_____

_____

_____

_____

_____

How can you do this thing to glorify God?_____

_____

_____

_____

_____

_____

_____

_____

EVALUATION

1. Whose ministry started first, Jesus' or John's?_____

2. Name three things John did to draw attention away from himself and toward Jesus. _____

_____

_____

_____

_____

3. Describe what happened during the period of overlap between Jesus' and John's ministries._____

_____

_____

4. What did John do that landed him in prison? _____

_____

5. How did John die? _____

_____

_____

Water into Wine

OVERVIEW

Jesus' ministry was the beginning of the new creation, and on the seventh day He revealed His glory at a wedding feast by turning ceremonial water into wine. By this miracle, Jesus demonstrated that the New Covenant was a covenant of celebration. As a result, His disciples believed in Him.

SOURCE MATERIAL

- John 2:1-11

ACTIVITIES

1. Have a Party. If you had a class party, in a short paragraph, write some of your thoughts about the it. _____

_____

_____

_____

Why was it important to have more than enough drinks at the party?_____

_____

_____

_____

_____

Why does God want us to celebrate under the New Covenant?_____

_____

_____

_____

_____

2. The Servants' Perspective. Imagine that you were one of the servants at the wedding and that Jesus instructed you to help with His miracle.

Would you feel excited to be a part of it? _____

_____

_____

_____

Would you think that the directions Jesus gave you were strange or perhaps unnecessary? _____

_____

_____

_____

_____

How would you feel once seeing the result of Jesus' miracle? _____

_____

_____

_____

_____

EVALUATION

1. In what way did the water of the Old Covenant differ from the water of the New Covenant?_____

_____

_____

_____

2. John presents the beginning of Jesus' ministry as the first seven days of the new creation. On what day did the water to wine miracle take place? _____

3. What is the significance of the seventh day, and why was it appropriate for this particular miracle?

_____

_____

_____

4. What are the symbolic meanings for water and wine? _____

_____

_____

5. What was the purpose of the pots that Jesus used for turning water into wine? _____

_____

_____

6. What message did Jesus send by turning ceremonial water into wine? _____

_____

_____

_____

7. What is the significance of Jesus performing this miracle at a wedding? _____

_____

•_____

8. Before Jesus performed this miracle, He told Mary that His "hour had not yet come." Why did He do the miracle anyway? _____

_____

From Darkness to Light: Jesus and Nicodemus

OVERVIEW

Jesus traveled to Jerusalem for the Passover feast and really kicked His ministry into high gear. He created a stir in the temple by running out the money changers and began preaching and performing miracles. Many believed in Him, but Jesus would not entrust Himself to them. One of the untrustworthy folks who believed in Jesus because of the signs, Nicodemus, came to Jesus at night to inquire further into His message and mission. Jesus began by explaining the necessity of the new birth, which set up His explanation of His unique qualifications and mission to save the world and invite people into fellowship with God.

SOURCE MATERIAL

- John 2:13-3:21
- Numbers 21
- Psalms 16-17
- Proverbs 12:15-16

ACTIVITIES

1. Think it Through. Answer the following question as best as you can and be prepared to discuss your findings in class. (For some Old Testament help, see Psalms 16-17 and the promises God made to Abraham in Genesis 12:1-3.)

Why did Jesus expect Nicodemus to already know that a person needs to be born again in order to enter the kingdom of God? _____

_____

_____

_____

_____

_____

2. Draw It. In the space below, draw an illustration that captures the analogy between the snake on a stick and Jesus on the cross (see John 3:14 and Numbers 21). Use your imagination.

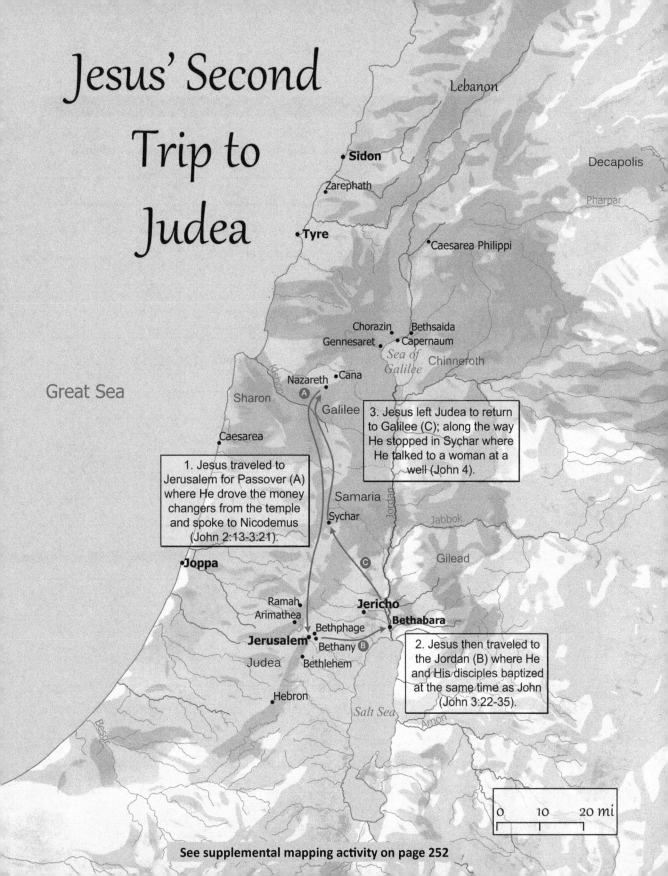

Jesus' Second Trip to Judea

Lebanon

Decapolis

Pharpar

Sidon

Zarephath

Tyre

Caesarea Philippi

Chorazin • Bethsaida

Gennesaret • Capernaum

Sea of Galilee Chinneroth

Nazareth • Cana

Ⓐ

Galilee

Great Sea

Sharon

Caesarea

1. Jesus traveled to Jerusalem for Passover (A) where He drove the money changers from the temple and spoke to Nicodemus (John 2:13-3:21).

3. Jesus left Judea to return to Galilee (C); along the way He stopped in Sychar where He talked to a woman at a well (John 4).

Samaria

Sychar

Jordan

Jabbok

Ⓒ

Gilead

Joppa

Ramah • Arimathea

Jericho

Bethabara

Bethphage

Jerusalem Bethany Ⓑ

Judea Bethlehem

Hebron

2. Jesus then traveled to the Jordan (B) where He and His disciples baptized at the same time as John (John 3:22-35).

Salt Sea

Arnon

Besor

0   10   20 mi

See supplemental mapping activity on page 252

EVALUATION

1. Why did Jesus cause such a ruckus in the temple, running out the money changers and animal sellers?_____

_____

_____

2. Why would Jesus not entrust Himself to those who believed in Him? _____

_____

_____

_____

3. What did Nicodemus think of Jesus before the conversation started? _____

_____

_____

4. Why does a person have to be born again in order to enter the kingdom of God? _____

_____

_____

5. What is the point of comparison that Jesus was driving at in John 3:14? _____

_____

_____

_____

_____

6. What was the challenge to Nicodemus in John 3:19-21? _____

_____

_____

_____

_____

Translation of John 2:1-21

*Singular uses of "you" are in plain text. Plural uses are in bold. For example, verse 7 should be read "Do not marvel that I said to you, '**You** (plural) must be born again.'"*

¹There was a man of the Pharisees named Nicodemus, a ruler of the Jews. ² This man came to Jesus by night and said to Him, "Rabbi, we know that You are a teacher come from God; for no one can do these signs that You do unless God is with him."

³ Jesus answered and said to him, "Most assuredly, I say to you, unless one is born again, he cannot see the kingdom of God."

⁴ Nicodemus said to Him, "How can a man be born when he is old? Can he enter a second time into his mother's womb and be born?" ⁵ Jesus answered, "Most assuredly, I say to you, unless one is born of water and the Spirit, he cannot enter the kingdom of God. ⁶ "That which is born of the flesh is flesh, and that which is born of the Spirit is spirit. ⁷ "Do not marvel that I said to you, '**You** must be born again.' ⁸ "The wind blows where it wishes, and you hear the sound of it, but cannot tell where it comes from and where it goes. So is everyone who is born of the Spirit."

⁹ Nicodemus answered and said to Him, "How can these things be?"

¹⁰ Jesus answered and said to him, "Are you the teacher of Israel, and do not know these things? ¹¹ "Most assuredly, I say to you, We speak what We know and testify what We have seen, and you do not receive Our witness. ¹² "If I have told **you** earthly things and **you** do not believe, how will **you** believe if I tell **you** heavenly things? ¹³ "No one has ascended to heaven but He who came down from heaven, that is, the Son of Man who is in heaven. ¹⁴ "And as Moses lifted up the serpent in the wilderness, even so must the Son of Man be lifted up, ¹⁵ "that whoever believes in Him should not perish but have eternal life. ¹⁶ "For God so loved the world that He gave His only begotten Son, that whoever believes in Him should not perish but have everlasting life. ¹⁷ "For God did not send His Son into the world to condemn the world, but that the world through Him might be saved.

¹⁸ "He who believes in Him is not condemned; but he who does not believe is condemned already, because he has not believed in the name of the only begotten Son of God. ¹⁹ "And this is the condemnation, that the light has come into the world, and men loved darkness rather than light, because their deeds were evil. ²⁰ "For everyone practicing evil hates the light and does not come to the light, lest his deeds should be exposed. ²¹ "But he who does the truth comes to the light, that his deeds may be clearly seen, that they have been done in God."

The Woman at the Well

OVERVIEW

Jesus met a Samaritan woman at Jacob's well and offered her living water. After a brief conversation with Jesus, she believed He was the Messiah, drank deeply of the living water, and went to tell her whole town about the man she met at the well. The disciples had also drank of that water but failed to tell a single person in Sychar that the Messiah stood just outside their town by the well. Jesus issued a challenge to them: eat the food of God—do His will and join in the harvest.

SOURCE MATERIAL

- John 4:1-42

ACTIVITIES

1. Journal Time 1. Write a paragraph in your journal or the space below about a person (or group of people) you know who is like the Samaritan woman (an outcast whom others look down upon). Write some specific ways you can make this person feel welcome in the family of God despite their differences or past failures just like Jesus did for the Samaritan woman. This person could be an unpopular kid at school, a difficult neighbor, a family member or an entire group such as the homeless or people of a different race_____

_____

_____

_____

_____

_____

_____

_____

_____

2. Journal Time 2. Jesus described obedience to God's will as "food" or satisfying to the soul. Write in your journal or the space below reflecting on the following.

Think of a time when you obeyed God's will. Describe the situation and write how it was satisfying to you._____

_____

_____

_____

_____

_____

Think of a time when you did not obey God's will. Describe the situation and write how it was dissatisfying._____

_____

_____

_____

_____

_____

Jesus said, "The harvest truly is great, but the laborers are few" (Luke 10:2). It is always God's will for us to be workers in the harvest field. Pray for God to reveal a "harvest field" where you can work with Him, thus doing His will and being satisfied with His "food."_____

_____

_____

_____

_____

_____

3. Act it Out. Act out the story of the woman at the well using the script. The following characters will be included in the skit: narrator, Jesus, woman, disciples (at this point Jesus only had five disciples: Peter, Andrew, John, Philip and Nathaniel), and the people of Sychar. Use the script below.

Narrator: Now Jesus learned that the Pharisees had heard that He was gaining and baptizing more disciples than John—although in fact it was not Jesus who baptized, but His disciples. So He left Judea and went back once more to Galilee. Now He had to go through Samaria. So He came to a town in Samaria called Sychar, near the plot of ground Jacob had given to his son Joseph. Jacob's well was there, and Jesus, tired as He was from the journey, sat down by the well. It was about noon when a Samaritan woman came to draw water.

Jesus: Give Me a drink?

Woman: [surprised] How is it that You, being a Jew, ask a drink from me, a Samaritan woman?

Jesus: If you knew the gift of God, and who it is who says to you, 'Give Me a drink,' you would have asked Him, and He would have given you living water.

Woman: [incredulously] Sir, You have nothing to draw with, and the well is deep. Where then do You get that living water? Are You greater than our father Jacob, who gave us the well, and drank from it himself, as well as his sons and his livestock?

Jesus: Whoever drinks of this water will thirst again, but whoever drinks of the water that I shall give him will never thirst. But the water that I shall give him will become in him a fountain of water springing up into everlasting life.

Woman: [sarcastically] Sir, give me this water, that I may not thirst, nor come here to draw.

Jesus: Go, call your husband, and come here.

Woman: [slightly saddened] I have no husband.

Jesus: You have well said, 'I have no husband,' for you have had five husbands, and the one whom you now have is not your husband; in that you spoke truly.

Woman: [amazed] Sir, I perceive that You are a prophet. Our fathers worshiped on this mountain, and you Jews say that in Jerusalem is the place where one ought to worship.

Jesus: [with authority] Woman, believe Me, the hour is coming when you will neither on this mountain, nor in Jerusalem, worship the Father. You worship what you do not know; we know what we worship, for salvation is of the Jews. But the hour is coming, and now is, when the true worshipers will worship the Father in spirit and truth; for the Father is seeking such to worship Him. God is Spirit, and those who worship Him must worship in spirit and truth.

Woman: [questioningly, as though she suspects He might be the Messiah] I know that Messiah is coming. When He comes, He will tell us all things.

Jesus: [boldly] I who speak to you am He.

Narrator: Just then His disciples returned and were surprised to find Him talking with a woman. But no one asked, "What do You seek?" or "Why are You talking with her?"

Disciples: [Return to the well and see Jesus talking with the woman, just as the woman begins to leave.]

Woman: [Leaving her water jar, goes back to the town and tells the people] Come, see a man who told me all things that I ever did. Could this be the Christ?

Townspeople: [Start walking out of the town towards Jesus. Many are talking excitedly. Townspeople freeze and stop talking as the attention is drawn back to Jesus and the disciples at the well.]

Peter: Rabbi, eat.

Jesus: *I* have food to eat of which *you* do not know. [put emphasis on the *I* and the *you*, Jesus is issuing a mild rebuke]

Philip: [confusedly speaking to the other disciples] Has anyone brought Him anything to eat?

Jesus: *My* [again, emphasis here to bring out the rebuke] food is to do the will of Him who sent Me, and to finish His work. Do you not say, 'There are still four months and then comes the harvest'? Behold, I say to you, lift up your eyes and look at the fields, for they are already white for harvest. And he who reaps receives wages, and gathers fruit for eternal life, that both he who sows and he who reaps may rejoice together. For in this the saying is true: 'One sows and another reaps. I sent you to reap that for which you have not labored; others have labored, and you have entered into their labors.

Townspeople and Woman: [walking along the path to the well and talking excitedly about the Messiah]

Narrator: Many of the Samaritans from that town believed in Him because of the woman's testimony, "He told me all that I ever did." So when the Samaritans came to Him, they urged Him to stay with them, and He stayed two days. And because of His words many more became believers. They said to the woman, "Now we believe, not because of what you said, for we ourselves have heard Him and we know that this is indeed the Christ, the Savior of the world."

[Script is adapted from NKJV]

EVALUATION

1. Why did the Jews hate the Samaritans so much? _____

_____

_____

_____

_____

2. Where in the Old Testament have we seen "woman at the well" stories? _____

_____

_____

3. What do these stories have in common? _____

_____

4. How does this scene with Jesus and the Samaritan woman fulfill those Old Testament pictures? ____

_____

_____

_____

_____

5. What does the fact that this woman had had five husbands tell us about her? _____

_____

6. What is the "living water" that Jesus was offering to the woman? _____

_____

7. When she believed in Jesus what did she immediately begin to do? _____

_____

8. How were the disciples doing on this point? _____

_____

9. What is the "food" that Jesus told His disciples about? _____

_____

UNIT 3   **3**   **JESUS' POPULARITY GROWS**

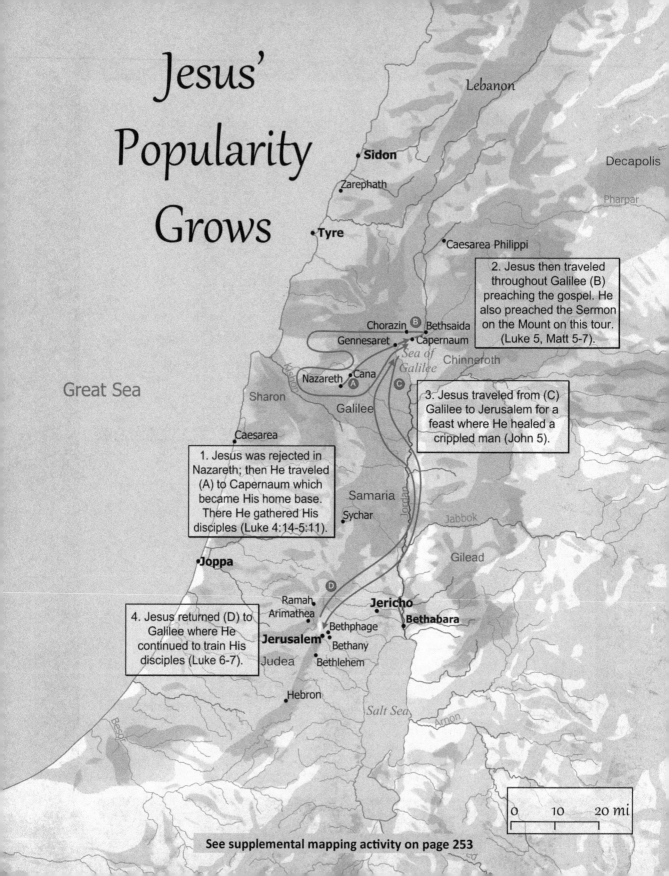

Jesus' Popularity Grows

Lebanon

Decapolis

• **Sidon**

Zarephath

Pharpar

• **Tyre**

• Caesarea Philippi

Chorazin (B) Bethsaida
Gennesaret • Capernaum

Chinneroth

Sea of Galilee

2. Jesus then traveled throughout Galilee (B) preaching the gospel. He also preached the Sermon on the Mount on this tour. (Luke 5, Matt 5-7).

Nazareth • Cana (A) (C)

Sharon

Great Sea

Galilee

3. Jesus traveled from (C) Galilee to Jerusalem for a feast where He healed a crippled man (John 5).

Caesarea

1. Jesus was rejected in Nazareth; then He traveled (A) to Capernaum which became His home base. There He gathered His disciples (Luke 4:14-5:11).

Samaria

Sychar

Jabbok

Gilead

• **Joppa**

(D)

Ramah
Arimathea

Jericho

4. Jesus returned (D) to Galilee where He continued to train His disciples (Luke 6-7).

Bethphage

Bethabara

Jerusalem • Bethany

Judea

Bethlehem

Hebron

Salt Sea

Arnon

0   10   20 mi

See supplemental mapping activity on page 253

Galilean Preaching and the Call by the Sea

OVERVIEW

Having returned by way of Samaria to Galilee, Jesus launched His Galilean ministry in earnest. Most of Jesus' ministry took place in Galilee where He preached the gospel, cast out demons, and healed diseases. He traveled from town to town, announcing deliverance and the coming of the kingdom everywhere He went. He began in His hometown, Nazareth, where He was rejected for not playing by their rules. He moved to Capernaum which became His home base. Jesus spent time in Capernaum, gathering disciples who would walk with Him throughout His earthly ministry.

SOURCE MATERIAL

- **Luke 4:14-5:11**
- Matthew 4:12-25, 8:14-17
- Mark 1:14-39

ACTIVITIES

1. Act it Out. Act out Luke 4:14-30. Your teacher will designate an area of the classroom to be the synagogue and another area to be the cliff outside of the town. Make sure you act out the people's transition from being amazed at Jesus because they hoped He would be their hometown hero, to hating Jesus and trying to kill Him because He was there to save the world, not only them. You will need the following characters:

- Jesus
- The synagogue attendant
- The people

2. Journal Time: Need for Jesus. In order to really experience what Jesus has to offer, we must recognize our deep need for Him. Spend some time writing in your journal or the space below, considering the following (see next page):

Do you come to Jesus recognizing your need for Him or do you think He owes you something for some reason? _____

_____

_____

If you lack that sense of your own need for Jesus, ask God to help you recognize your need for Him; He gives generously to all without finding fault._____

_____

_____

_____

EVALUATION

1. Was Jesus already a known figure in Galilee before He returned there to begin His ministry? How did people know of Him?_____

_____

_____

_____

2. According to the Old Testament passage that Jesus read in Nazareth, what was His ministry all about?_____

_____

_____

3. Why did the people of Nazareth reject Jesus?_____

_____

_____

4. Where did Jesus go after He was rejected in Nazareth? _____

_____

5. Which disciples did Jesus call in Capernaum?_____

_____

Jesus' Miracles Demonstrated that He is a Greater Priest

OVERVIEW

Jesus is a new and greater priest from a greater priesthood. Instead of inspecting a leper to see if he was clean as the Law directed, Jesus declared the man clean while he was still leprous. The word of Jesus made the man clean. Likewise, Jesus declared a sinner forgiven without requiring him to offer the requisite sacrifices, and He proved His power to do so by healing the man of his paralysis. Both of these acts offended the established religious authorities, but that wasn't all. Following these miracles, Jesus went and partied with a tax collector without fear that He would dirty himself by doing so. Jesus is truly a greater priest.

SOURCE MATERIAL

- **Luke 5:12-5:39**
- Matthew 8:1-4, 9:1-17
- Mark 1:40-2:22

ACTIVITIES

1. Research Assignment. Research what a Jewish tax collector did in Jesus' day and why they were hated by the rest of the Jews.

Why would Jesus call a tax collector as a disciple? _____

_____

_____

Why do you suppose Matthew (Levi) was so eager to follow Jesus? _____

_____

_____

What might have made him throw such a big party on that occasion?_____

_____

_____

2. Journal Time: A Greater Priesthood. Jesus is the beginning and head of a greater priesthood, a priesthood where the broken are declared clean, sins are forgiven, and life and light is shone to all around. We are priests in the line of Jesus and are called to perform these same priestly duties in the world just like Jesus did. Answer the following questions in your journal or in the space provided.

Is there someone in your life who needs to know that Jesus has the power to bring physical or emotional health? How can you pray for and encourage this person?_____

_____

_____

_____

_____

Is there someone in your life who needs to know that Jesus loves and forgives him? How can you share Christ's forgiveness with that person?_____

_____

_____

_____

_____

_____

What are some ways you can be a source of life and light to those around you?_____

_____

_____

_____

_____

_____

_____

EVALUATION

1. How did the manner in which Jesus pronounced the leper clean differ from how the priests at the temple did the same? _____

_____

_____

2. How did the healing of the man with leprosy present a claim of Jesus' authority to the priests? ____

_____

_____

3. How did the manner in which Jesus forgave the paralyzed man differ from how priests at the temple forgave? _____

_____

4. How did Jesus demonstrate that His forgiveness of the paralyzed man was genuine? _____

_____

5. What do the two miracles in Luke 5 (cleansing the leper and forgiving the paralyzed man) demonstrate about Jesus?_____

_____

6. Why did the two miracles Jesus performed in Luke 5 (cleansing the leper and forgiving the paralyzed man) present a threat to the established religious authorities? _____

_____

_____

_____

_____

7. How did the calling of Matthew and the feast that followed challenge the Jewish leaders? _____

_____

_____

_____

The Sermon on the Mount

OVERVIEW

During His early Galilean ministry, Jesus preached the Sermon on the Mount, the archetypal sermon that Jesus would preach to His disciples during this part of His ministry. In this sermon, Jesus, the ultimate Son of God, taught God's many other sons how to relate to their *good* Father. Jesus taught Christians how to relate to the Law, how to pray, fast and give, encouraged them not to worry and promised that their good Father was eager to answer their prayers. He concluded with an explanation of how difficult being His disciple would be and included some signposts to look for along the way to know they remained on the path.

SOURCE MATERIAL

- Matthew 5:1-7:29

ACTIVITIES

1. Who Are You in the Story? Jesus was surrounded by eager disciples, nominal followers, hostile crowds and antagonistic religious people. Imagine that you lived in Galilee during Jesus' time and consider where you would have fit into this story. Would you have been on that mountainside listening attentively to Jesus? Would you have been up close to Jesus or in the back row? Would you have thought all this excitement about Jesus was just hype and would have rather stayed home? Or would you have been an antagonist—only there to try to get some dirt on Jesus? Spend some time thinking about these questions and write a short paragraph explaining your thoughts below._____

_____

_____

_____

_____

_____

_____

_____

The Sermon on the Mount is a call to move closer to Jesus. Is Jesus asking you to move closer to Him? If Jesus is calling you to be a closer follower, tell that to Jesus: tell Him that you want what He has to offer. _____

_____

_____

_____

_____

2. Jesus and the Law. Read Matthew 5:21-32, then write a short answer to each of the following questions regarding the Law. Be prepared to discuss your answers.

Jesus interpreted the Old Testament laws prohibiting murder, adultery and divorce. Does His explanations of these laws make them more difficult to keep or easier? _____

_____

_____

_____

With the command against murder, as it was normally interpreted, it was pretty easy to measure how you were doing: if you never killed a person, you hadn't broken it. How do you measure your progress under Jesus' interpretation of it? _____

_____

_____

_____

I thought Jesus was here to bring good news, but His interpretation of the Law sounds hopelessly impossible for those who want to know they are being good Christians. What's the deal?_____

_____

_____

_____

What can we do to find peace if we look inside ourselves and only find a sinner?_____

_____

_____

3. Classroom Discussion Questions. Answer the following questions and be prepared to discuss them with the class.

What kind of things do you tend to worry about? Do you think God cares about those things and wants to meet those needs? How can you know that God is going to provide in that area?_____

_____

_____

_____

_____

Jesus said, "Judge not, that you be not judged" (Matt 7:1). Does this mean we should never point out someone else's sin?_____

_____

_____

What are we supposed to do before we help a brother out of a sin? _____

_____

_____

_____

Jesus said that it's easy to end up on the road to destruction and difficult to stay on the path of life. What does Jesus' discussion following this statement indicate that we can do to help keep us on the path?_____

_____

_____

_____

_____

_____

_____

_____

EVALUATION

1. What was Jesus trying to accomplish with the Sermon on the Mount? _____

_____

_____

2. Did Jesus have very many followers at this point?_____

_____

3. What are the Beatitudes all about? _____

_____

_____

4. Are the blessings of the Beatitudes for now or later? _____

5. Does Jesus make measurable obedience to the Law more difficult or easier?_____

_____

_____

6. Why is it a bad idea to pray and fast in order to gain the approval of others? _____

_____

_____

7. How can we know that God is going to meet our needs? _____

_____

_____

8. That whole narrow path thing makes the Christian life sound difficult; what are some things you can do to make sure you stay on the path? _____

_____

_____

_____

_____

_____

Jesus Healed a Crippled Man in Jerusalem

OVERVIEW

Jesus went to Jerusalem and picked up where He had left off in His confrontation with the Pharisees, priests and teachers of the law. Jesus healed a disabled man on the Sabbath as a way to demonstrate to the religious leaders *who He was*. The man He healed had been in his condition for 38 years, just like the first generation wandered in the wilderness for 38 years. And like that generation, he lived in a temporary "house of grace" awaiting salvation. Jesus reenacted the deliverance of Israel when they entered the promised land by healing this man during the Feast of Tabernacles (or Booths). This healing set the stage for a confrontation with the religious leaders who accused Jesus of working on the Sabbath. Jesus didn't argue with them; He went along with it and claimed that He worked on the Sabbath because His Father was at work too. Elaborating on this, Jesus told them that they could expect a lot more from Him because the Father had given Him a lot to do.

SOURCE MATERIAL

- John 5:1-47

ACTIVITIES

1. Testimonies of Jesus. We should not believe a person's claims about himself based only on his own testimony. He needs someone else to testify about him or have evidence to back up his claims. Read John 5:31-46 and answer the following questions.

Make a list of all the different evidences that Jesus says testify about Him in John 5:31-46._____

_____

_____

_____

_____

_____

_____

Make a list of some other testimonies about Jesus, not included in John 5:31-46._____

_____

_____

_____

_____

_____

Which evidence do you find most convincing and why?_____

_____

_____

_____

_____

_____

_____

_____

2. Act it Out. Your teacher will divide your class into two groups to act this story out. Below are the instructions for the two different groups.

The first group is to act out the stirring of the Bethesda pool. Your teacher will assign a handicap to several of you and will designate an area of the classroom as the pool. One of you will be the angel who stirs the water of the pool. While the angel stirs the water, those of you who are invalids must try to make it into the pool first.

The second group is to act out Jesus' interaction with the lame man and the healed man's interaction with the religious leaders. Use the text in John 5:5-15 as a script.

EVALUATION

1. Why doesn't John say what feast this was? _____

_____

2. What feast was it and what clues does John give to help get us there?_____

_____

_____

_____

_____

3. Why would sick and disabled people collect by this pool? _____

_____

4. Why had the man not been healed there after 38 years?_____

5. What did Jesus ask him before He healed him?_____

6. What did Jesus say to the man to heal him? _____

7. On what day did this miracle occur? _____

8. How did the religious leaders respond when they saw the man walking? _____

_____

9. What did the religious leaders say to Jesus when they found out He had healed the man?_____

_____

10. How did Jesus respond to their accusation? _____

_____

11. Why was Jesus pushing the religious leaders so hard?_____

_____

12. What did Jesus say about His relationship with the Father? _____

_____

13. What was the one testimony that the religious leaders really should have heard and received? ____

_____

Jesus Chose and Taught His Disciples

OVERVIEW

Jesus had been agitating the religious leaders throughout His Galilean ministry and even more so when He went to Jerusalem. His disciples were starting to catch on, and they imitated Jesus by plucking grain on the Sabbath—therefore breaking one of the rules of the religious leaders. Jesus saw this as a good sign; His followers were starting to do what He did. So He chose twelve and called them apostles; these were the ones He was going to send out *to do the same kinds of things He had done—miracles and all*. After teaching His disciples, Jesus performed two of the greatest miracles that He had done to date—healing a man from a distance and raising a widow's son from the dead. Imagine what His apostles who were going to be sent out to do these kinds of things might have been thinking! Jesus was preparing His followers to do great things.

SOURCE MATERIAL

- Luke 6:1-7:17

ACTIVITIES

1. Journal Time. Spend some time thinking, praying and writing about the following in your journal or in the space below:

Jesus could confront the Pharisees because He loved them first. He also waited until He had matured and earned the respect of the people. Think of a person or group of people that you wish you could confront like Jesus confronted the Pharisees. Now spend some time praying that God would give you the ability to love this person (or people) the way Jesus loved people. Write out your prayer for this person (or people). _____

_____

_____

_____

_____

_____

2. Classroom Discussion: Becoming the Superhero. After your class discussion on superheros, reflect on the activity and write what you learned in the space below._____

_____

_____

_____

_____

_____

_____

_____

_____

_____

_____

EVALUATION

1. Did the disciples know that it would frustrate the religious leaders when they plucked grain on the Sabbath? _____

_____

_____

2. Then why did they do it? _____

_____

_____

3. When Jesus responded to the religious leaders, He compared Himself and His disciples to David and his companions. What was He trying to get across by this comparison? _____

_____

_____

4. Why do you think Jesus chose His twelve apostles right after this? _____

_____

_____

5. What is the main difference between the Sermon on the Plain in Luke and the Sermon on the Mount in Matthew? _____

_____

_____

_____

6. Why do you think Jesus might have followed His choosing of the apostles with such great miracles?

_____

_____

7. What do you think the apostles might have been thinking when Jesus raised the dead? _____

_____

_____

UNIT 4   **4**   JESUS REJECTED

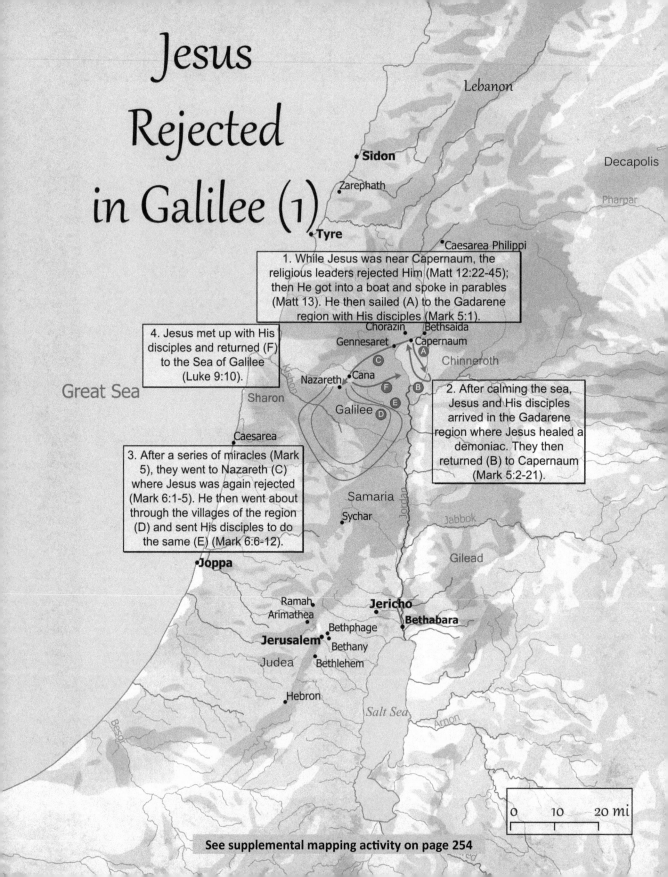

Jesus Rejected in Galilee (1)

Lebanon

Decapolis

Pharpar

Sidon

Zarephath

Tyre

Caesarea Philippi

1. While Jesus was near Capernaum, the religious leaders rejected Him (Matt 12:22-45); then He got into a boat and spoke in parables (Matt 13). He then sailed (A) to the Gadarene region with His disciples (Mark 5:1).

Chorazin   Bethsaida

Gennesaret   Capernaum

Chinneroth

4. Jesus met up with His disciples and returned (F) to the Sea of Galilee (Luke 9:10).

Great Sea

Nazareth   Cana

Sharon

Galilee

2. After calming the sea, Jesus and His disciples arrived in the Gadarene region where Jesus healed a demoniac. They then returned (B) to Capernaum (Mark 5:2-21).

Caesarea

3. After a series of miracles (Mark 5), they went to Nazareth (C) where Jesus was again rejected (Mark 6:1-5). He then went about through the villages of the region (D) and sent His disciples to do the same (E) (Mark 6:6-12).

Samaria

Sychar

Jabbok

Gilead

Joppa

Ramah

Arimathea

Bethphage

Jericho

Bethabara

Jerusalem

Bethany

Judea   Bethlehem

Hebron

Salt Sea

Arnon

0   10   20 mi

See supplemental mapping activity on page 254

The Turning Point: Galilee Rejected Jesus

OVERVIEW

Jesus' message had divided His audience; His closest disciples were firmly committed to Him, and many crowds were following Him; but the religious establishment was ready to reject Him. The religious leaders were capable of casting out demons, but believed that only the Messiah could cast out a mute demon. When Jesus accomplished this feat, they attributed His ability to Beelzebub, the prince of demons. Jesus rebuked them for blaspheming the Holy Spirit and called them to repent. This represented a turning point in Jesus' ministry; the nation, that generation of Israel, had rejected the Messiah. Jesus in turn rejected them and moved to build a new people out of His followers.

SOURCE MATERIAL

- **Matthew 12:22-12:45**
- Mark 3:22-35
- Jonah 3
- Psalm 32

ACTIVITIES

1. Compare and Contrast: Ninevites and Pharisees. Read Jonah 3 and Matthew 12:31-32. Then, on the next page, make a list of as many similarities and differences between the Ninevites and Pharisees as you can.

Ninevites	Pharisees

2. Repentance Psalm. Sing or read Psalm 32 which is one of David's psalms of repentance. Spend some time praying and reflecting on this psalm; then write your prayers and repentance in your journal or in the space below._____

_____

_____

_____

_____

_____

_____

3. Theological Discussion. After your class discussion about the abundance of forgiveness answer the following questions.

What does Romans 5:20 teach about the forgiveness that Jesus purchased for us on the cross?_____

_____

_____

_____

_____

_____

_____

Explain why Saul/Paul is such a powerful example of God's abundant grace and forgiveness._____

_____

_____

_____

_____

_____

EVALUATION

1. Why did Jesus seek to prove to the religious leaders that He was the Messiah? _____
_____
_____

2. What point was Jesus making when He healed a mute demoniac? _____
_____
_____

3. What is blasphemy against the Holy Spirit?_____
_____
_____

4. Why is blasphemy against the Holy Spirit a bigger deal than blasphemy against the Son of Man?____
_____
_____
_____

5. Why did Jesus call the religious leaders to Himself to reason with them; what was He hoping to get
out of the conversation? _____
_____

   What was He calling them to repentance for? _____
_____
_____

6. The individuals who committed blasphemy against the Holy Spirit were called to repentance;
beyond that, what did their rejection of Jesus mean for the nation?_____
_____
_____

7. How did Jesus respond to the national rejection of Him? To whom did He turn? _____
_____

OVERVIEW

Having been rejected by the religious leaders, Jesus turned His attention to His followers through whom He would now bring the kingdom. Jesus began speaking in parables so that His followers would understand what He was saying, but the truth would be hidden from those who rejected Him. The parables in Matthew 13 are descriptions of what was happening to the kingdom during Jesus' lifetime more than they are principles of how the kingdom would operate in the apostolic age. Israel, as a nation, had rejected the kingdom, and so Jesus planned to bring the kingdom to earth through His followers as a "new people."

SOURCE MATERIAL

- Matthew 12:46-13:52

ACTIVITIES

1. **Study the Soils.** Jesus described four types of soils in His first parable (Matt 13:3-9, 18-23). The first (the path) represents soil that never sprouted life: unbelievers. The last (the fruitful soil) is what we are all aiming for. The two in the middle—the rocky soil and the thorny soil—teach us a lot about the temptations we will face in life that could pull us off the path of the righteous. Answer the following questions regarding the rocky and thorny soils.

What temptations does the rocky soil warn us about? _____

_____

What does the plant in rocky soil need in order to prevent being uprooted when these trials come? ___

_____

What would "deeper roots" look like in your life? _____

_____

What temptations does the soil that produces thorns warn you about? _____

_____

What are some examples of "thorns" or worldly temptations that you might face in your life?_____

_____

_____

What can you do to prepare for these temptations, so that they will not deceive you?_____

_____

_____

_____

2. Journal Time. In your journal or the space below, write down a temptation/trial that you are struggling with or think you might struggle with in the future. Write down what you can do to protect yourself from that temptation._____

_____

_____

_____

_____

_____

_____

_____

_____

3. Interpret the Parables. Your teacher will assign you a parable. As a group, figure out what this parable means and answer the questions below. You will then explain the parable to the whole class.

Parable Title:_____

1. What does each major character or object in the parable represent?_____

_____

_____

_____

_____

_____

_____

2. What is the meaning of the parable?_____

_____

_____

_____

_____

_____

_____

_____

EVALUATION

1. What are parables? _____

_____

_____

2. In general, what are the kingdom parables about? _____

_____

_____

_____

3. Describe two truths that help in interpreting the parables._____

_____

_____

4. Explain the meaning of one of the parables._____

_____

_____

_____

Jesus Built His Disciples' Faith

OVERVIEW

Having been rejected by the religious leaders, Jesus began to focus on building His disciples' faith. Jesus displayed the greatness of His power by calming a storm—demonstrating that He had power over creation, and by casting a "legion" of demons out of a man—demonstrating that He had power over the entire demonic realm. Following these miracles, a synagogue leader named Jairus asked Jesus to come heal his daughter. Along the way, Jesus was distracted when He *felt* power go out from Him to heal someone in the crowd. After He found out who caused this, Jesus commended her for her faith and continued on His way. By the time He arrived to heal Jairus' daughter, she was already dead. Jesus invited His three closest disciples into the room and raised her from the dead. Soon afterward, He arrived at His hometown, but was unable to perform very many miracles there because of their lack of faith.

SOURCE MATERIAL

- Mark 4:35-6:6

ACTIVITIES

1. Act it Out. As a group, your job is to write a skit and act out one of the four stories from this lesson. Emphasize the disciples' response when Jesus performed the miracles. The four stories are:

- Jesus calmed the storm (Mark 4:35-41).
- Jesus restored a demon-possessed man (Mark 5:1-20).
- Jesus raised a dead girl and healed a sick woman (Mark 5:21-43).
- Jesus returned to Nazareth (Mark 6:1-6).

2. Implications of Jesus' Miracles. Jesus used miracles to teach truths about Himself. Answer the following questions, using Mark 4:35-5:43 as a reference.

What does the fact that Jesus calmed the storm tell us about Jesus?_____

_____

_____

Jesus didn't pray and ask God to calm the storm, He directly commanded the storm to be still. What is the difference between simply praying for a miracle and commanding a miracle to happen? _____

_____

_____

When Jesus arrived on the other side of the sea, a man with thousands of demons came and fell on his knees before Him and made requests of Jesus. What does this tell us about Jesus?_____

_____

_____

In the story of Jairus' daughter, Jesus didn't pray that God would heal her, He simply commanded her to stand up. What does this tell us about Jesus?_____

_____

_____

3. Faith Stretcher. In the space below or in your journal, write of a time when God did something miraculous in your life or in the life of someone you know. _____

_____

_____

_____

_____

_____

_____

_____

_____

EVALUATION

1. Now that Israel had rejected Him, Jesus focused on training His disciples. In this lesson, what was the specific aim Jesus had for His disciples' growth?_____

_____

_____

2. Why is it important to "fear" Jesus as a part of increasing your faith in Him?_____

_____

_____

3. What does the fact that Jesus calmed the storm with a simple command tell us about who Jesus is?

_____

_____

4. What does Jesus' interaction with the demon-possessed man tell us about Jesus' relationship to the demonic forces? _____

_____

_____

5. What does Jesus' raising of Jairus' daughter tell us about Him? _____

_____

_____

6. How might the disciples have felt seeing this aggressive sequence of miracles? _____

_____

_____

7. What is the connection between the faith of the people and Jesus' ability to perform miracles?_____

_____

_____

_____

_____

Jesus Sent Out the Twelve Apostles

OVERVIEW

Jesus gave the twelve apostles authority over demons and sent them out to do what He had been doing. But this was more than just a "trial run"; Jesus gave them authority to accept or reject cities and individuals on behalf of the kingdom. In short, if the city accepted them, the city was accepted; and if the city rejected them, they were to dust off their feet and depart from the city as though Jesus Himself had rejected it. Meanwhile, Jesus' reputation as a powerful and important man was being established at higher levels. In this lesson, we learn how Herod heard about Jesus and understood that something important was going on with Him.

SOURCE MATERIAL

- **Mark 6:6-31**
- Matthew 10:1-42

ACTIVITIES

1. Act it Out. Your teacher will split your class into two groups; each group will have a different skit to act out. Each group is to use Jesus' instructions to His apostles to help them create their skit (shown below). Also, follow the directions for your specific group.

- Don't go to Gentiles or Samaritans, only to the lost sheep of Israel (Matthew 10:5-6).
- Preach the message: "The kingdom of heaven is at hand" (Matthew 10:7).
- Heal the sick, raise the dead, cleanse lepers, drive out demons (Matthew 10:8).
- Don't take provision with you (Matthew 10:9-10, Mark 6:8-9).
- In each town, seek to find a welcoming place and let your peace rest on it if it is worthy; if it is not worthy, let your peace return (Matthew 10:11-13, Mark 6:10).
- If a place will not welcome you, shake the dust off your feet as a sign of judgment (Matthew 10:14-15, Mark 6:11).

Group 1: Town of Welcome. Your job is to perform a skit in which two apostles go to a town that welcomes the kingdom. Assign two people to act as apostles and the other people in your group can be townspeople. Remember the instructions (shown below) that Jesus gave to His apostles and make sure to incorporate these into your skit, if they apply. Use your imagination, and have fun!

Group 2: Town of Rejection. Your job is to perform a skit in which two apostles go to a town that rejects the kingdom. Assign two people to act as apostles and the other people in your group can be townspeople. Remember the instructions (shown below) that Jesus gave to His apostles and make sure to incorporate these into your skit. Use your imagination, and have fun!

2. Journal Time. Our lives here on earth are about much more than simply going about our daily tasks or leading a successful life in the world's eyes. We are to be like the apostles—sent out to share the good news of the kingdom. Spend some time thinking and praying about how God wants to use your life for the kingdom like He used the lives of the apostles. Then, write in your journal or in the space below. You can write your prayers or write your convictions on how God might be leading you._____

_____

_____

_____

_____

_____

_____

_____

_____

_____

_____

_____

_____

_____

EVALUATION

1. Jesus' closest disciples had been following Him since early in His Galilean ministry, but when did Jesus really start training them to be apostles? _____

_____

2. What does the word "apostle" mean?_____

3. When the twelve were sent out, what, in essence, was their task?_____

_____

_____

4. To whom were the twelve sent? _____

_____

5. What message were they to preach in the towns they went into? _____

_____

6. What were they to do if a town didn't welcome them?_____

_____

7. What did the apostles actions towards the unwelcoming town mean? _____

_____

The Feeding of the 5,000

OVERVIEW

Jesus worked a miracle and became very popular for the wrong reasons. In order to continue on His mission without being encumbered by an army of 5,000 men trying to make Him king, Jesus challenged their spiritual dullness, offended them, and even drove away a number of His disciples as a result.

SOURCE MATERIAL

- **John 6:1-71**
- Matthew 14:13-33
- Mark 6:32-52
- Luke 9:10-17

ACTIVITIES

1. Dramatic Re-Enactment. As a group, your job is to re-enact the dialogue between Jesus and the crowd, starting in John 6:25 and going through John 6:59. Instead of just reading the biblical text though, put the text into your own words and do your best to make the story clear to a modern audience.

2. Journal Time: Trusting God. The twelve disciples chose to trust Jesus even though they didn't understand everything He was saying. Think of a time in the past or of a current situation where you didn't understand what God was doing. In your journal or the space below, write about this situation and, if God later made His purposes clear to you, write about that too. Then write a prayer to God, asking Him to help you trust Him even when you don't understand._____

_____

_____

_____

_____

Journal Time (cont.)_____

_____

_____

_____

_____

EVALUATION

1. How did Jesus set up the feeding of the 5,000?_____

_____

_____

_____

2. How much food was left over? _____

3. How did the crowd respond?_____

4. What did Jesus do about that response? _____

5. Where did the feeding take place, and where did the crowd catch up to Jesus?_____

_____

_____

6. How did Jesus respond to the crowd when they caught up to Him? _____

_____

_____

7. What did Jesus do when the crowd misunderstood Him? _____

_____

_____

8. Why didn't Jesus explain Himself at least to His disciples? _____

_____

_____

_____

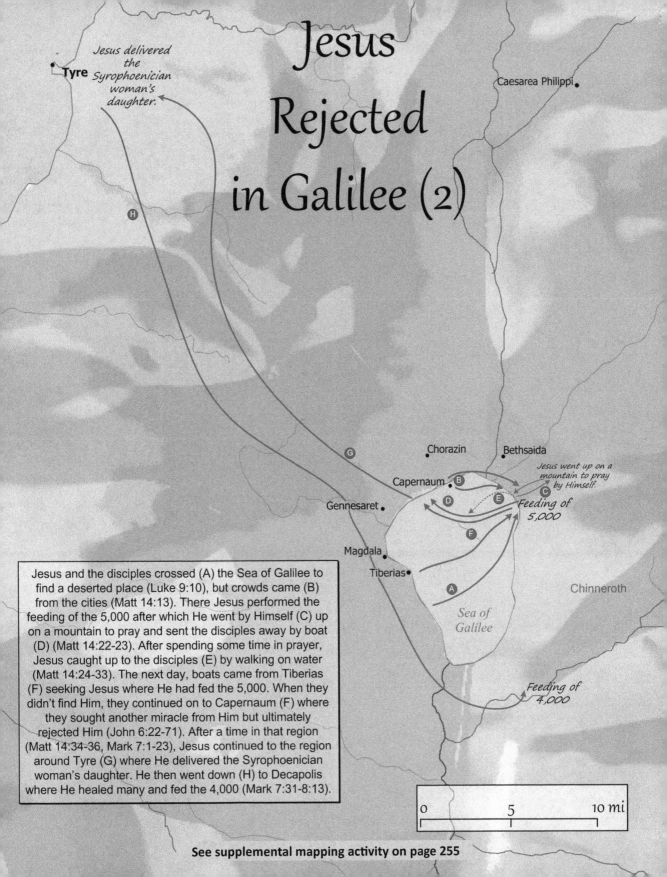

Jesus Rejected in Galilee (2)

Tyre
Jesus delivered the Syrophoenician woman's daughter.

Caesarea Philippi.

H

Chorazin
Bethsaida

Jesus went up on a mountain to pray by Himself.

G

Capernaum
B
C

Gennesaret
D
E
Feeding of 5,000

F

Magdala

Tiberias

A

Chinneroth

Sea of Galilee

Feeding of 4,000

Jesus and the disciples crossed (A) the Sea of Galilee to find a deserted place (Luke 9:10), but crowds came (B) from the cities (Matt 14:13). There Jesus performed the feeding of the 5,000 after which He went by Himself (C) up on a mountain to pray and sent the disciples away by boat (D) (Matt 14:22-23). After spending some time in prayer, Jesus caught up to the disciples (E) by walking on water (Matt 14:24-33). The next day, boats came from Tiberias (F) seeking Jesus where He had fed the 5,000. When they didn't find Him, they continued on to Capernaum (F) where they sought another miracle from Him but ultimately rejected Him (John 6:22-71). After a time in that region (Matt 14:34-36, Mark 7:1-23), Jesus continued to the region around Tyre (G) where He delivered the Syrophoenician woman's daughter. He then went down (H) to Decapolis where He healed many and fed the 4,000 (Mark 7:31-8:13).

0   5   10 mi

See supplemental mapping activity on page 255

Miraculous Healings and the Feeding of the 4,000

OVERVIEW

Jesus continued to build the disciples' faith in different areas: their treatment of the religious leaders, their understanding of praying in faith, and their trust for God's provision.

SOURCE MATERIAL

- **Matthew 14:34-15:39**
- Mark 6:53-8:9
- John 7:1

ACTIVITIES

1. Purity Before God. The Pharisees had a long list of ways to maintain purity before God. Washing hands before eating was just one of them. Jesus told the disciples that external cleanliness isn't how purity really works; it's about what is in the heart. We might not have the same list that the Pharisees had, but in our culture, we have our own set of traditions that we use instead of really addressing the sins in our hearts (see Matt 14:19 for a handy list). In the space below, brainstorm a list of the things people use as substitute sources of purity rather than dealing with their sin. _____

_____

_____

_____

2. A Big, Stupid Prayer. Think about some of the problems you face in your life. In the Lord's Prayer, Jesus said, "Thy kingdom come; Thy will be done on earth as it is in heaven." What would it look like for God's kingdom to break out right there in the middle of your biggest problem? In the space provided on the following page, or in your journal, write a prayer asking God's kingdom to come in the midst of your problem. It can feel like a stupid thing to pray for, but Jesus praised the Canaanite woman for taking her big request and just asking over and over until He did it.

_____

_____

_____

_____

_____

_____

EVALUATION

1. What were the Pharisees known for?_____

2. How did old people get taken care of in Jesus' society? Nursing homes? Social Security payments?__
_____

3. What tradition of the Pharisees did Jesus criticize? _____
_____

4. Why did Jesus criticize the Pharisees' tradition? _____
_____

5. Did Jesus intend for the disciples to go off on an anti-Pharisee crusade?_____
_____
_____

6. What was the point Jesus was making to the crowd?_____
_____

7. Why did Jesus say that the Canaanite woman had great faith?_____
_____

8. Compare and contrast the feedings of the 5,000 and the 4,000. What was the same? What was
different?_____
_____
_____
_____

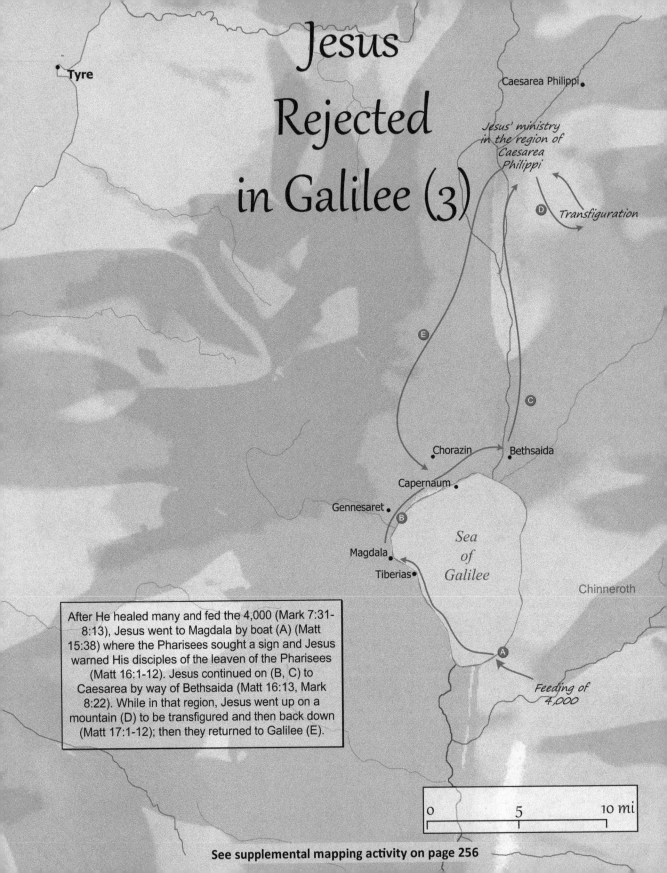

Jesus

Rejected

in Galilee (3)

Tyre

Caesarea Philippi

Jesus' ministry in the region of Caesarea Philippi

Ⓓ *Transfiguration*

Ⓔ

Ⓒ

Chorazin   Bethsaida

Capernaum

Gennesaret

Ⓑ

Sea of Galilee

Magdala

Tiberias

Chinneroth

After He healed many and fed the 4,000 (Mark 7:31-8:13), Jesus went to Magdala by boat (A) (Matt 15:38) where the Pharisees sought a sign and Jesus warned His disciples of the leaven of the Pharisees (Matt 16:1-12). Jesus continued on (B, C) to Caesarea by way of Bethsaida (Matt 16:13, Mark 8:22). While in that region, Jesus went up on a mountain (D) to be transfigured and then back down (Matt 17:1-12); then they returned to Galilee (E).

Ⓐ

Feeding of 4,000

| 0 | 5 | 10 mi |

See supplemental mapping activity on page 256

The Leaven of the Pharisees

OVERVIEW

Jesus had been training His disciples to trust the Father for provision, but they hadn't really gotten the message. In this lesson, Jesus connected the dots for them.

SOURCE MATERIAL

- **Matthew 15:39-16:12**
- Mark 8:10-21

ACTIVITIES

1. Worrying about Following God's Leading. One of the major lessons in this passage is to trust God to provide for your needs wherever He leads you. Unlike people in Jesus' day, you probably don't have to worry about starving in the desert before you can reach the next town. In the space below, answer the following questions.

What are some worries you face or could see yourself facing in the future?_____

_____

_____

_____

_____

_____

What might God ask you to do, and what might you worry about when you step out to do it? _____

_____

_____

_____

_____

2. The Teaching of the Pharisees and Sadducees. While most Christians are not in particular danger today of believing what the Pharisees taught 2,000 years ago, we still have false teachers today. Answer the following questions.

Name some false teachers and false teachings that happen today._____

_____

_____

_____

_____

_____

How are we in danger of absorbing this teaching?_____

_____

_____

_____

_____

_____

How can we protect ourselves from absorbing this false teaching?_____

_____

_____

_____

_____

_____

_____

_____

_____

_____

EVALUATION

1. How did people feel about the Pharisees in Jesus' time? _____
_____

2. Why did the Pharisees ask Jesus for a sign? _____
_____
_____

3. Why did Jesus refuse to give them a sign? _____
_____
_____
_____

4. What one sign did Jesus offer? _____
_____

5. Why did Jesus call His death and resurrection "the sign of the prophet Jonah"? _____
_____
_____

6. Why did Jesus need to warn His disciples about the Pharisees' teaching?_____
_____
_____
_____

7. Why did the disciples think Jesus was talking about them forgetting bread? _____
_____
_____
_____

8. How did Jesus correct them?_____
_____
_____

The Transfiguration: Peter Learned About the Path to Glory

OVERVIEW

Peter was in tune with the Father and was able to boldly say that Jesus was the "Messiah, the Son of the living God" (Matt 16:16, NIV). But he didn't get the principle of baptism: that true life came through death. When Jesus told His disciples that He must suffer and die, Peter rebuked Him and then received a harsh rebuke from Jesus. Jesus taught them that the way of the cross was the way of discipleship and then gave His three closest disciples a foretaste of what His glory would look like.

SOURCE MATERIAL

- Matthew 16:13-17:13

ACTIVITIES

1. Write a Short Story. Jesus taught that a person must go through a cross experience, a genuine trial, before being glorified. Our culture tells us, "You are great; you can do anything you set your mind to and easily overcome any obstacle." Your job is to write two different short stories, a self-made hero story (the one our culture tells us is true) and a way-of-the-cross story (the one Jesus says is true). Some instructions are given below.

- Each story should be about one page long, but the way-of-the-cross story will be slightly longer than the self-made hero story.
- In both stories, the basic plot is: a knight conquers a dragon to rescue the princess and marry her.
- In the first story, the knight is so awesome that he is able to defeat the dragon with no problem. Every step of the way confirms his awesomeness.
- In the second story, the knight goes through some terrible ordeal either before facing the dragon that makes him capable of defeating the dragon, or during the process of defeating the dragon. He must find help outside of himself, either by bringing to life a truth that he has learned from someone else but never understood before, or by depending on something outside of himself to make it through the ordeal. In either case, he must sustain some kind of injury in the process of defeating the dragon.

Bonus: Draw an illustration for each of your stories.

First Story (self-made hero story): _____

_____

_____

_____

_____

_____

_____

_____

_____

_____

_____

_____

_____

_____

_____

_____

_____

_____

_____

_____

_____

_____

_____

_____

_____

Second Story (way-of-the-cross story):_____

_____

_____

_____

_____

_____

_____

_____

_____

_____

_____

_____

_____

_____

_____

_____

_____

_____

_____

_____

_____

_____

_____

_____

_____

_____

_____

2. Journal Time: View of Trials. Before this lesson, spend some time writing in your journal or the space below about questions 1 and 2. After this lesson, answer questions 3 and 4.

1. Do you generally view trials/difficulties as good or bad things? Explain your answer._____

_____

_____

_____

_____

2. Describe a difficult experience you've had or are currently having. Did or do you think of this particular experience as a good or bad thing?_____

_____

_____

_____

_____

3. What did Jesus teach about difficulties or trials? How does He want us to think of our trials?_____

_____

_____

_____

_____

3. Look back at the difficult experience you wrote about at the beginning of class. How does what Jesus taught about trials change the way you think about this experience?_____

_____

_____

_____

_____

EVALUATION

1. How did Peter know that Jesus was the Messiah, the Son of God?_____

_____

2. Why did Jesus have to suffer and die?_____

_____

_____

3. What biblical symbol teaches us that suffering precedes glory? _____

_____

4. Why did Jesus respond so sharply to Peter's rebuke?_____

_____

_____

5. What was the Transfiguration demonstrating to the disciples who were there?_____

_____

_____

6. Why did Peter want to build houses for Jesus, Moses and Elijah at the Transfiguration, and what did this reveal about him?_____

_____

_____

Jesus Taught the Disciples About Greatness

OVERVIEW

When the disciples failed to cast out a demon, Jesus taught them about faith and prayer. Their failure drove home the point better than success ever could have. As they continued on, Jesus taught them that true greatness would require them to humble themselves and become like little children, which would mean losing confidence in themselves and learning to trust in God. The path to greatness passes through failure and requires childlike humility and faith.

SOURCE MATERIAL

- Matthew 17:14-18:35

ACTIVITIES

1. Children and Greatness. Jesus taught that true greatness required being like a child. Make a list of characteristics children have that Jesus might have had in mind._____

_____

_____

_____

_____

_____

What are some practical ways you can live more like a child as Jesus taught?_____

_____

_____

_____

_____

_____

2. Journal Time: Fear of Failure. Spend some time writing in the space below or in your journal about how the fear of failure can stop you from doing the things God wants you to do. Answer the following questions.

Why does fear of failure often stop us from doing what God wants us to do?_____

_____

_____

_____

_____

Why does God not want us to be afraid of failure? What are some things that we can learn through failure?_____

_____

_____

_____

Write about something you are afraid of doing because you are afraid of failing. Ask God to give you the courage to do what He wants you to, even if you might fail at it._____

_____

_____

_____

_____

_____

_____

_____

_____

_____

EVALUATION

1. Why were the disciples unable to cast the demon out of the boy who was brought to them? _____

_____

_____

2. Why is trying to do something good and failing better than not trying at all?_____

_____

_____

_____

3. How is failure related to the way of the cross? In other words, why is failure found on the path to glory?_____

_____

_____

4. How is being like a child a good thing for a Christian?_____

_____

_____

_____

UNIT 5   **5**   JESUS' FINAL DAYS

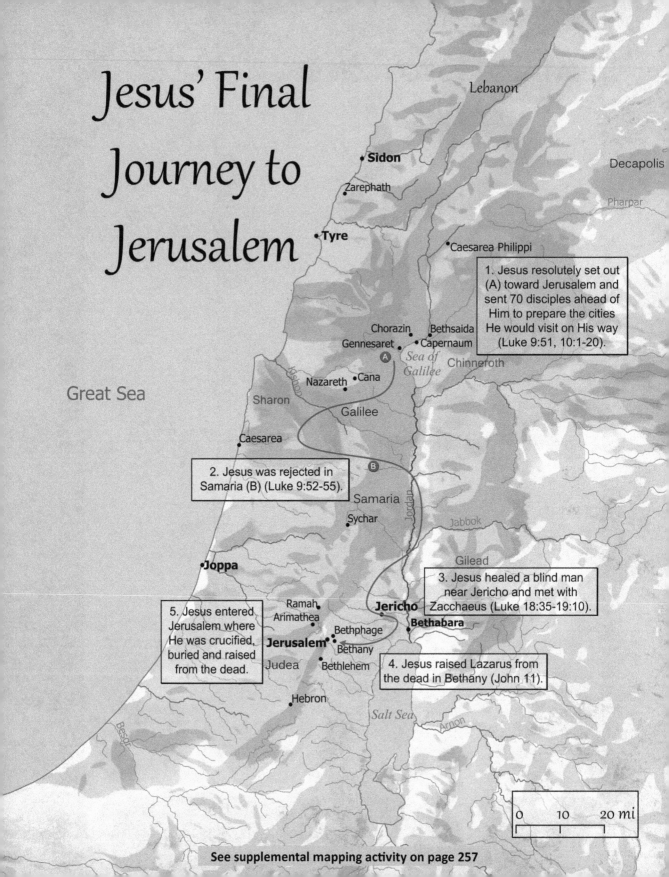

Jesus' Final Journey to Jerusalem

Lebanon

Decapolis

Sidon

Zarephath

Pharpar

Tyre

Caesarea Philippi

1. Jesus resolutely set out (A) toward Jerusalem and sent 70 disciples ahead of Him to prepare the cities He would visit on His way (Luke 9:51, 10:1-20).

Chorazin   Bethsaida

Gennesaret   Capernaum

(A)   *Sea of Galilee*   Chinneroth

Nazareth   Cana

Great Sea

Sharon

Galilee

Caesarea

(B)

2. Jesus was rejected in Samaria (B) (Luke 9:52-55).

Samaria

Sychar

Jabbok

Gilead

Joppa

3. Jesus healed a blind man near Jericho and met with Zacchaeus (Luke 18:35-19:10).

Ramah

5. Jesus entered Jerusalem where He was crucified, buried and raised from the dead.

Arimathea

Jericho

Bethphage   **Bethabara**

Jerusalem   Bethany

Judea   Bethlehem

4. Jesus raised Lazarus from the dead in Bethany (John 11).

Hebron

Salt Sea   Arnon

Besor

0   10   20 mi

See supplemental mapping activity on page 257

The Sending of the Seventy and the Fall of Satan

OVERVIEW

Jesus set His face resolutely toward Jerusalem; He was going there to die. As He made His way throughout the land and even into Gentile territories, He sent out seventy of His disciples to announce His coming and give the people a final chance to repent. This was to fulfill the parable of the wheat and tares. His disciples returned with joy because they had power over demons. Jesus rejoiced with them, for their victory wasn't just earthly; He saw Satan fall from heaven. He validated His disciples' excitement, but told them to take the most joy in the fact that their names were recorded in heaven.

SOURCE MATERIAL

- Luke 9:51-10:24

ACTIVITIES

1. Act Out the Spiritual Realities. In this lesson we get a glimpse into the significance of our actions. When we are doing the work of God, a battle is going on in the heavenly places. When we pray for someone, speak out in the name of Christ, or perform an act of love in His name, we are taking part of a spiritual battle that is much bigger than the visible situation. As a group, your job is to act out the spiritual battles that happen when we do God's work. Come up with a story of everyday Christian love such as giving food and prayer to a homeless person or encouraging a hurting friend in the name of Christ. Be creative, but make sure that you are (1) doing an act of true love and (2) doing it in Jesus' name. At the same time as some of your group is acting out the story of Christian love, the rest of your group is to act out the spiritual battle in the heavenly realm. You will have two scenes going at once, but they should be parallel or related to each other. You will be asked to act out your story in front of the class.

2. Write a Short Story. In the space provided below, write a short story (1/2 page to a page long) from the perspective of one of the seventy disciples whom Jesus sent out. Include the disciples' experience in one of the towns they visited. The story should also convey the joy and excitement the disciples felt at the success of their mission. _____

_____

_____

_____

_____

_____

_____

_____

_____

_____

_____

_____

_____

_____

_____

_____

_____

_____

_____

_____

EVALUATION

1. Why would James and John think it was a good idea to call down fire on the Samaritan village? Why were they wrong?_____

_____

_____

_____

_____

_____

2. Why did Jesus send the seventy through Israel at this point?_____

_____

_____

3. Why would the success of the seventy cause Satan to fall from heaven?_____

_____

_____

_____

4. What are we called to do in the world? _____

_____

_____

5. What is significant about Jesus sending His disciples out twice? _____

_____

_____

Related to this, what is the significance of the numbers twelve and seventy? _____

_____

_____

Jesus Raised Lazarus from the Dead

OVERVIEW

To the disciples' consternation, Jesus headed to Judea a couple of days after He heard that His friend Lazarus was dead. The disciples were concerned that Jesus could get Himself killed in Judea. When He arrived in Bethany, Lazarus was already dead. Martha, Lazarus' sister, really wanted Jesus to raise him from the dead. Jesus assured her that *He* was the resurrection and the life, but stopped short of clearly saying that He was going to raise Lazarus from the dead. Jesus then met with Mary and joined in her mourning. When they arrived at the tomb, Jesus called Lazarus out, and he came. Many were in awe at this miracle, but some reported it to the religious leaders in Jerusalem who plotted all the more to kill Jesus.

SOURCE MATERIAL

- **John 11:1-54**
- Luke 10:38-42
- Psalm 16:10

ACTIVITIES

1. Draw Lazarus. In the space provided below, draw a picture of Lazarus coming out of the grave still wrapped in his grave clothes (or perhaps in the process of unwrapping them). You can include additional details if you would like such as the open tomb, Jesus and the crowds, etc.

2. Act it Out: The Story of Lazarus. As a class, your job is to act out the story in John 11:1-54. Think through the fact that real people actually experienced this—they saw someone raised from the dead. Imagine the shock and awe! You should fill the following roles:

- Narrator
- Jesus
- The disciples
- Mary
- Martha
- Lazarus
- The crowds
- Naysayers
- God-praisers

You can use your Bible as a script. The narrator will read everything surrounding the direct quotations, while the actors act out what the narrator reads. When a direct quote is in the text, the actors should read that.

EVALUATION

1. What did Jesus mean when He said, "This sickness will not end in death" (John 11:4)?_____

_____

_____

_____

2. Why did Jesus wait until Lazarus had died before He went to Bethany?_____

_____

_____

3. Why was Martha so eager to approach Jesus and say that she knew God would do anything He asked?_____

_____

4. How did Jesus respond to her pressing request?_____

_____

_____

_____

5. What did Jesus do when He saw Mary's pain at the loss of her brother?_____

6. Everyone was expecting there to be a stench after the stone was rolled away from Lazarus' tomb; how do we know that there wasn't a smell?_____

_____

_____

_____

7. What was the effect of Jesus thanking the Father that there was no stench? _____

_____

_____

8. What kind of response did this miracle provoke?_____

_____

Jesus' Arrival in Jerusalem

OVERVIEW

Jesus entered Jerusalem triumphantly on a donkey, as a king victorious on the battlefield, returning to sit on His throne. But instead of going to a palace, He went to the temple where He was challenged by the religious leaders of Israel. He easily answered their questions and turned their attempted traps back on them. Jesus rebuked the leaders of Israel and cried for the loss of His city.

SOURCE MATERIAL

- **Matthew 21:1-23:39**
- Mark 11:1-12:40

ACTIVITIES

1. Dramatic Reading. Jesus really went after the Pharisees and teachers of the law in Matthew 23:13-39, but He was speaking out of love, out of the pain of loss. We often don't think of love and anger going together, but this was the way it was for Jesus. His love is especially evident in the last paragraph (Matthew 23:37-39). Following the dramatic reading of this passage in class, write down some of your reflections and be prepared to share these thoughts with the class. _____

_____

_____

_____

_____

_____

_____

_____

_____

_____

2. Understanding the Traps. You will be assigned a group and one of the following three passages. In your group, read and discuss the following questions about the passage together. Then, a representative from your group will share your responses with the rest of the class.

Passages:

- Matthew 22:15-22
- Matthew 22:23-33
- Matthew 22:34-40

1. What were the religious leaders expecting Jesus to say in response to their question?_____

_____

_____

_____

_____

_____

2. How could that question have trapped Jesus?_____

_____

_____

_____

_____

_____

3. How did Jesus surprise them to undermine the trap?_____

_____

_____

_____

_____

_____

_____

EVALUATION

1. What does it mean that Jesus rode into Jerusalem on a donkey? _____

_____

_____

_____

2. How did the crowds respond to this?_____

_____

3. What was the meaning of Jesus causing the fruitless fig tree to wither? _____

_____

_____

4. Jesus had had many clashes with the religious leaders. What was different about this clash? _____

_____

_____

5. How did Jesus respond to the question of the religious leaders who were attempting to trap Him?

_____

_____

6. What is the general meaning of the parables that Jesus directed to the religious leaders?_____

_____

_____

_____

7. What was the main emotion behind Jesus' woes upon the Pharisees?_____

_____

_____

Jesus Instituted Communion

OVERVIEW

Jesus' final time of fellowship with His disciples was the Passover meal, a meal with a rich history of communion with God. Jesus transformed that meal from a memorial of the exodus to a memorial of God's deliverance through Jesus Christ. When we partake of communion, we are feasting with God and enjoying the blessing of the future in the midst of our present wandering.

SOURCE MATERIAL

- **Luke 22:3-20**
- Matthew 26:14-29
- Mark 14:10-25
- John 13-17

ACTIVITIES

1. With a Smile On. Answer the following questions about how your church does communion.

Is it presented as a happy or sad event? _____

_____

_____

What kind of music is played before, during and after?_____

_____

_____

What kind of behavior is expected during communion? (examples are bowing your head, meditating on your sins, singing, clapping hands, etc.)_____

_____

_____

We don't want you to be critical of your church, but we do want you to be aware of the attitude you have about the Lord's table. Next time your church does communion, think consciously about communion as a meal with the Lord. As you partake of it, thank the Lord, smile as though you are at a feast with friends and raise your head up, even if you need to keep your eyes closed. After doing these things at a communion service, write two to three sentences in response to the following question.

How did your joyful attitude change your experience of communion?_____

_____

_____

_____

_____

_____

2. The Meaning of Bread. Bread is an ancient food staple with a rich history and symbolism. Use the Internet or other resources you may have to research the history and symbolism of bread. Remember, the Internet can have some very helpful information, but don't believe everything you read there!

Write a few sentences about what you found on the history of bread._____

_____

_____

_____

_____

_____

Write a few sentences on the possible symbolism or meaning of bread._____

_____

_____

_____

_____

_____

What might have been some of the reasons why Jesus chose bread to be His body in the communion meal?_____

_____

_____

_____

EVALUATION

1. What do the tree of life, Passover, the peace offering and communion all have in common?_____

_____

_____

2. How is communion related to Passover?_____

_____

_____

3. What is the meaning of bread in the world?_____

_____

4. What is the meaning of wine in the world?_____

_____

5. Why would Jesus want us to eat His flesh and drink His blood?_____

_____

Jesus Betrayed, Arrested and Forsaken

OVERVIEW

Jesus went to the garden of Gethsemane on the Mount of Olives to prepare for His arrest. He prayed in earnest to the Father while His disciples slept. Judas came and betrayed Him, and Jesus willingly went before the religious leaders to be accused so that He might obey God to the point of death.

SOURCE MATERIAL

- **Matthew 26:36-75**
- Psalm 55

ACTIVITIES

1. The Passion. After watching a clip from The Passion of the Christ, write your reflections and feelings in your journal or in the space below._____

_____

_____

_____

_____

_____

_____

_____

_____

_____

_____

_____

2. Journal Time: Pray for Protection. Jesus spent time praying the night before His arrest. We too will face trials and temptation. It is important to learn to pray for protection against giving in to temptation during times of trial. In your journal or the space below, spend some time writing out your prayer for protection against temptation. If you have a specific temptation you are currently struggling with, write about that; if you can't think of a specific temptation at this time, write for protection for the future._____

_____

_____

_____

_____

EVALUATION

1. Why did Jesus ask for His cup to be taken away? Was He actually thinking of not going through with His death?_____

_____

2. What was the impact of the disciples' lack of vigilance during the time they should have been praying in the garden?_____

_____

3. Why did Peter cut off the servant's ear? What didn't he "get" that led to his violence?_____

_____

_____

4. Why did the religious leaders arrest Jesus at night?_____

_____

5. What kind of accusations were brought against Jesus? _____

_____

6. What happened to the disciples when Jesus was arrested?_____

_____

_____

Jesus Tried and Convicted

OVERVIEW

The religious leaders took Jesus before Pilate, while Judas committed suicide for betraying an innocent man. The religious leaders wanted Jesus dead more than anyone, but they didn't want to take responsibility for killing Him. Pilate didn't want to take responsibility either; Jesus, however, put Pilate in the position of deciding whether or not He was King of the Jews. After trying to pass the buck, Pilate finally complied with the wishes of the people and sent Jesus off to be crucified. Pilate washed his hands of the thing, while the people took responsibility for Jesus' blood.

SOURCE MATERIAL

- **Matthew 27:1-31**
- Luke 23:4-12

ACTIVITIES

1. The Passion. After watching a clip from The Passion of the Christ, write your reflections and feelings in your journal or in the space below._____

_____

_____

_____

_____

_____

_____

_____

_____

_____

2. Class Discussion: Responsible Parties. In this story there are many responsible parties to Jesus' death. Only the people and Judas took the blame, but many more had a hand in it. Fill in the table below, writing how each different person or group of people were guilty of Jesus' death and what they might have done differently.

Guilty Party	How were they guilty?	What could they have done differently?
Judas		
The Religious Leaders		
The People		
Pilate		
Herod		
The Roman Guards		
The Disciples		

3. Jesus Made King. In this lesson, we learned how the Roman soldiers mockingly made Jesus King; they didn't realize that their actions done in mockery were actually things that are true of Jesus. In groups, read Matthew 27:27-29 and list all the things the soldiers did in mockery to make Jesus King. Then, match each of the things the soldiers did with one of the verses below that predicts Jesus' kingship in a glorious, non-mocking way.

Genesis 49:10	**Revelation 14:14**
Philippians 2:10	**Revelation 19:13**

List of wast the soldiers mocked Jesus	Corresponding verse of Jesus Kingship

EVALUATION

1. In what way were the religious leaders like Judas? _____

_____

2. Pilate asked Jesus if He was King of the Jews and Jesus said, "You have said so" (Matt 27:11b, NIV). What was the effect of this? Was it an admission of being King?_____

_____

_____

3. What did Pilate do to avoid making a decision about Jesus? _____

_____

_____

4. What finally convinced Pilate to give the go-ahead to kill Jesus?_____

_____

5. Who ended up taking responsibility for Jesus' death?_____

_____

6. What happened to Jesus after Pilate sent Him off to be crucified?_____

_____

Jesus' Crucifixion and Burial

OVERVIEW

The entirety of the Old Testament points toward the coming Messiah as the final head-crusher. Jesus' disciples were expecting Jesus to defeat their enemies and take His rightful place as King. Instead, He was mocked, beaten, crucified and buried. He received the fate of the serpent in order to defeat the serpent once and for all.

SOURCE MATERIAL

- **Matthew 27:32-66**
- Mark 15:21-47
- Luke 23:26-56
- John 19:16-42

ACTIVITIES

1. The Passion. After watching a clip from The Passion of the Christ, write your reflections and feelings in your journal or in the space below._____

_____

_____

_____

_____

_____

_____

_____

_____

_____

_____

2. Painting Interpretation. In your groups, carefully examine the painting on page 177 of the moment that Christ died. Try and see the hidden meanings and symbolism in the painting and write down your thoughts. _____

_____

_____

_____

_____

_____

_____

_____

_____

_____

_____

EVALUATION

1. We all know the Bible well enough to know that the hero died right at the climax, but the disciples had no idea that this would happen—why?_____

_____

_____

2. Why did Jesus have to die to defeat the serpent? _____

_____

_____

3. How did the disciples see Jesus' death at the time? How did they see it after the resurrection? _____

_____

_____

4. What does Simon of Cyrene's act of carrying the cross teach us about discipleship_____

_____

Jesus' Resurrection and Ascension

OVERVIEW

The whole Bible points to the need for resurrection—for water to wash over all things and transform death into life. When Jesus' body was put in the grave, His disciples thought that the end of their hope had come, but it was only the beginning. Jesus rose from the dead and appeared to many; therefore, we have hope.

SOURCE MATERIAL

- **John 20:1-21:14**
- Matthew 28
- Mark 16
- Luke 24

ACTIVITIES

1. Journal Time: Walking in the Resurrection. Spend some time in prayer, asking God to reveal an area of death around you—anything that doesn't fit into God's kingdom—that needs resurrection. It might be a need for physical healing, a relational problem with your family or friends, or someone's need to hear the gospel. After hearing from the Lord, in the space below or in your journal write out a short (one or two sentence) specific prayer relating to that area. Then, pray that prayer every day until God answers it.

The area of death that needs resurrection:_____

_____

_____

My specific prayer:_____

_____

_____

_____

2. Hope of Heaven vs. Hope of the Resurrection. Individually, in groups, or as a class, answer the following questions about heaven and the resurrection.

What happens to people after they die? _____

_____

_____

_____

_____

What is heaven for? What are we going to do there? _____

_____

_____

_____

_____

Are we ever going to leave heaven, or is that our permanent home? _____

_____

_____

_____

_____

Will we ever be reunited with our bodies like Jesus was when He rose from the dead? Or will we forever be bodiless spirits in heaven?_____

_____

_____

_____

Read Revelation 21, and write down some of your thoughts about it below. Be prepared to discuss these thoughts as a class._____

_____

_____

_____

EVALUATION

1. The disciples were not expecting Jesus to die, and once He died, they didn't know that He would be resurrected. We wouldn't have gotten it had we been them, but what big hint in the Bible points toward Jesus' death and resurrection? _____

_____

_____

2. What does Jesus' resurrection mean for the serpent?_____

_____

_____

3. When did the disciples believe that Jesus had risen from the dead?_____

_____

_____

_____

4. Describe Jesus after the resurrection._____

_____

5. What does the resurrection mean for us?_____

_____

._____

6. Where will we go when we die?_____

7. Will we stay there forever? What happens next? _____

_____

UNIT 6 — 6 — THE CHURCH IS BORN

OVERVIEW

Jesus commissioned the disciples to go into the world, preach the gospel and bring all nations to Christ. This was an impossible calling for man, but Jesus promised the Holy Spirit would come to empower them to accomplish the mission. When the Holy Spirit came, the 120 Christians spoke in tongues and Peter preached a convicting sermon, leading 3,000 people to Christ. And thus, the Church began.

SOURCE MATERIAL

- Acts 1-2

ACTIVITIES

1. How to Wait. Read through Acts 1:12-26. In the space below, make a list of all the things the disciples did while they waited for the outpouring of the Holy Spirit. _____

_____

_____

_____

_____

_____

_____

_____

_____

_____

_____

In many ways you may also be in a period of waiting in your life; you may not yet know what your specific gifting and calling are. In the space below, make a list of some things you can do to wait wisely until you really know and act upon your calling._____

_____

_____

_____

_____

_____

_____

_____

2. Journal Time: Pray for Miracles. Spend some time in prayer, asking God to reveal ways you can be praying for miracles. These prayers may be requests for opportunities to share the gospel or pray for unbelievers, prayers for peace during difficult times, or prayers for God's provision. Make your prayer requests specific, pray faithfully for these miracles and thank God for them when they happen._____

_____

_____

_____

_____

_____

_____

_____

_____

_____

_____

_____

EVALUATION

1. What happened to the disciples when Jesus breathed on them in John 20?_____
_____
_____
_____

2. What is the difference between Jesus breathing on the disciples in John 20 and the outpouring of the Holy Spirit on Pentecost?_____
_____
_____
_____

3. What did the disciples do while they waited for the Holy Spirit to come upon them?_____
_____
_____

4. What is the gift of tongues in Acts 2?_____
_____
_____

5. Why do you think God might have given them that particular gift? _____
_____
_____

6. What was Peter's sermon all about?_____
_____
_____
_____

7. How many converted when Peter preached this sermon? _____

   What happened with all of these new converts?_____
_____

Peter and the Growing Church

OVERVIEW

Peter and John were imprisoned overnight for healing a lame man in the name of Jesus. The next day, a council of the religious leaders in Jerusalem convened to question them about this healing. Peter boldly proclaimed before the council that they healed the man in the name of Jesus whom those very religious leaders were guilty of crucifying. The council deliberated about what to do, but they were trapped. They could not deny the healing, since everyone knew about it, and they could not punish Peter and John for healing a lame man, so they decided to threaten and release them. Upon their release, Peter and John returned to their companions who immediately thought of Psalm 2 and began to pray. After they prayed, the house shook by the power of the Holy Spirit, and the Church redoubled their efforts in fellowship and mission.

SOURCE MATERIAL

- Acts 3-4
- Psalm 2
- Proverbs 30:5-6

ACTIVITIES

1. Class Discussion: Psalm 2 and What's Your Story? When the Church heard about Peter and John's victory against the council, they immediately began quoting Psalm 2. Discuss the significance of this psalm in groups or as a class. Then, think of a story from your life or a story from Church history where Psalm 2 would have been an appropriate song to sing in response. Write this story in the space below and explain why Psalm 2 would be an appropriate psalm in this situation._____

_____

_____

_____

_____

_____

_____
_____
_____
_____
_____
_____
_____
_____

2. Journal Time: Boldness for the Gospel. Consider whom God has placed in your life to share Christ's love with. Have you been bold in sharing the gospel, or has fear stopped you from doing so? Spend some time writing about this in the space below or in your journal. Then ask God for opportunities to share the gospel with this person and boldness to do so when these opportunities arise._____

_____
_____
_____
_____
_____
_____
_____
_____
_____
_____
_____
_____
_____

EVALUATION

1. What happened that led to Peter and John getting arrested?_____
_____
_____

2. What was it that bothered the religious leaders most about the healing?_____
_____
_____
_____

3. Why were the religious leaders not able to punish Peter and John?_____
_____
_____

4. What did Peter say when the religious leaders told them not to preach the name of Jesus? _____
_____
_____

5. Why did the Church sing Psalm 2 in response to what happened? _____
_____
_____
_____

6. Are you as bold as Peter is in sharing the gospel? Why or why not? _____
_____

The Stoning of Stephen

OVERVIEW

The Church was born into a volatile situation in Jerusalem. Many of the Jewish believers who had lived in Greek cultures (known as Hellenistic Jews), were just visiting Jerusalem when they heard the gospel. Many of these new Christians stayed in Jerusalem, which meant there was a need to share resources, food and living space and to take care of all the new believers. Unfortunately, some of the Hellenistic widows were being neglected. So the apostles appointed deacons to distribute the food fairly. Stephen, a Hellenist himself, was chosen as a deacon. He got into a dispute with some non-Christian Hellenistic Jews who falsely accused him and took him before the Sanhedrin. Stephen preached a convicting message against the religious leaders and was killed for it. His face shone like Moses, and he died innocent like Jesus. Stephen's death was the beginning of the expansion of the gospel in keeping with Jesus' commission in Acts 1:8.

SOURCE MATERIAL

- Acts 6-7

ACTIVITIES

1. Compare and Contrast. Stephen's sermon (Acts 6:8-7:52) bears a lot of similarities to Peter's sermon (Acts 2). Read through the passages and make a list of similarities and differences between the two sermons.

Similarities	Differences

2. Act it Out. Act out some or all of the story in this lesson (Acts 6-7). It is especially important to act out the actual stoning of Stephen. Make sure to include in your skit some of the things you don't really catch when reading the story: the anger (gnashing their teeth) of Stephen's attackers, the fact that they covered their ears and yelled while they attacked him, and, of course, Stephen's calm demeanor during his attack.

EVALUATION

1. What was going on in Jerusalem that necessitated appointing deacons?_____

_____

_____

_____

2. How did Stephen end up on trial before the Sanhedrin? _____

_____

_____

_____

3. Answer the following questions based on Stephen's sermon before the Sanhedrin:

What was the promise that God had made to Abraham?_____

_____

Why did God send Moses to the people of Israel?_____

_____

Did Israel receive Moses?_____

_____

What promise did Stephen point to?_____

_____

What was the punch line, the big point, Stephen ended with? _____

_____

_____

_____

4. What does the phrase "cut to the heart" mean? Talk about Acts 2 in your answer._____

_____

_____

_____

5. In what ways was Stephen like Jesus? _____

_____

_____

_____

The Church Persecuted and Scattered

OVERVIEW

Up until the martyrdom of Stephen, the gospel had basically stayed in Jerusalem. But after Stephen's death, a great persecution began against Christians, and the Church was scattered throughout Judea and Samaria (in keeping with Jesus' commission in Acts 1:8). We see the expansion of the gospel through the story of Philip's ministry, first in Samaria—healing, preaching and baptizing—and next in Judea where the Ethiopian eunuch was converted on his way home. Philip's is the first missionary journey we see in Acts, but there are many more to come. In fact, Philip was a precursor to the great missionary Paul.

SOURCE MATERIAL

- Acts 8

ACTIVITIES

1. Compare and Contrast. Fill in the following chart, listing the similarities and differences between Philip and Saul.

Similarities	Differences

What are some lessons you can take away from these similarities and differences? Be prepared to discuss your answer. _____

_____

_____

_____

_____

2. Journal Time: Scattered and Gathered. The Church is called to be both the scattered and the gathered people of God. Use the matrix and the questions below to evaluate your life, writing your thoughts in your journals or the space on the following page.

Cozy life – lots of time with God's people, rarely on mission

Fruitful life – cycle between gathering and scattering (work and rest)

Gathered – in worship

Scattered – on mission

Death – separated from God's people and God's mission

Stressed life – always doing, never resting

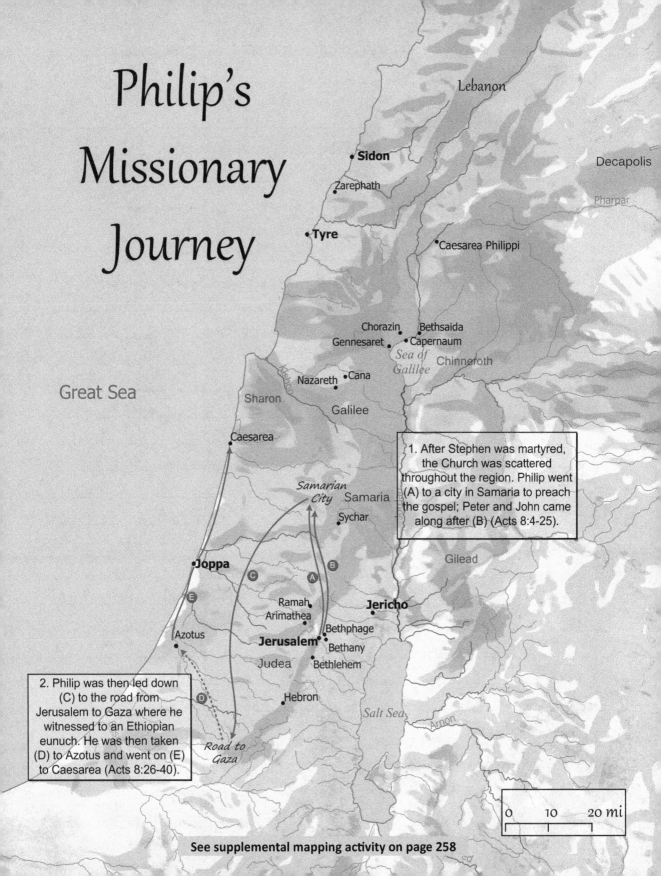

Philip's Missionary Journey

Lebanon

Decapolis

Sidon

Zarephath

Pharpar

Tyre

Caesarea Philippi

Chorazin   Bethsaida

Gennesaret   Capernaum

Sea of Galilee   Chinneroth

Nazareth   Cana

Great Sea

Sharon

Galilee

Caesarea

Samarian City   Samaria

Sychar

> 1. After Stephen was martyred, the Church was scattered throughout the region. Philip went (A) to a city in Samaria to preach the gospel; Peter and John came along after (B) (Acts 8:4-25).

Gilead

Ⓒ   Ⓐ   Ⓑ

Joppa

Ⓔ

Ramah   **Jericho**

Arimathea

Bethphage

Azotus   **Jerusalem**   Bethany

Judea   Bethlehem

> 2. Philip was then led down (C) to the road from Jerusalem to Gaza where he witnessed to an Ethiopian eunuch. He was then taken (D) to Azotus and went on (E) to Caesarea (Acts 8:26-40).

Ⓓ   Hebron

Salt Sea

Arnon

Road to Gaza

0   10   20 mi

See supplemental mapping activity on page 258

Are you the kind of person who tends toward the gathered community of God and neglects your mission?_____

What kind of temptations will that kind of person experience in their Christian life?_____

_____

_____

_____

_____

Are you the kind of person who likes to be doing stuff for God all the time and rarely pulls back to rest with God's people? _____

What kind of temptations will that kind of person experience in their Christian life?_____

_____

_____

_____

_____

What are some concrete steps you can take to move to a balanced and fruitful life?_____

_____

_____

_____

_____

_____

_____

_____

_____

_____

_____

_____

_____

EVALUATION

1. What did it take for the Church to begin spreading the gospel throughout Judea and Samaria as Jesus had called them to in Acts 1:8?_____

_____

_____

2. Describe how the story of Philip's travels and ministry points to Saul's future ministry._____

_____

_____

_____

3. What was Stephen's background and position in the Jerusalem church? _____

_____

4. Why do you think that God chose Hellenistic deacons to be on the front lines of the gospel expansion while the apostles remained at Jerusalem? After all, didn't Philip have important work to do in Jerusalem? _____

_____

_____

_____

_____

_____

5. Were the Samaritans and the Ethiopian eunuch Gentiles? Explain your answer._____

_____

_____

6. Philip left Jerusalem to spread the gospel. Why did Saul leave Jerusalem?_____

_____

The Conversion of Saul

OVERVIEW

Saul was on a missionary journey to persecute Christians when he met Christ in a flash of light. After Jesus spoke to Saul, his heart was open to the truth of the gospel, but his eyes were blinded. He went on to Damascus where he met Ananias, was baptized, and his eyes were opened. Immediately, Saul began preaching the gospel, though to little great effect. Finally, he journeyed to Jerusalem and made peace with the apostles, laying the groundwork for a powerful ministry.

SOURCE MATERIAL

- Acts 9:1-31

ACTIVITIES

1. Compare and Contrast. Using Acts 8 and 9 (Lessons 6.4 and 6.5), compare and contrast Saul with the Ethiopian eunuch.

Saul	Ethiopian Eunuch

What lessons can you take away from this comparison? Be prepared to discuss your answer in class.

_____

_____

_____

_____

_____

_____

_____

_____

_____

2. Journal Time: Repentance. Think of a time God attempted to give you a course correction, but you simply treated it as a speed bump. Pray and ask the Lord to tell you an area in your lives (even a small area) where you need to repent. Write about this in the space below or in your journal.

_____

_____

_____

_____

_____

_____

_____

_____

_____

_____

_____

_____

_____

EVALUATION

1. What was Saul doing while Philip was seeking to spread the gospel out from Jerusalem? _____

_____

_____

2. What happened to Saul when he met Jesus on the road to Damascus? _____

_____

_____

3. How did Saul behave after his conversion? _____

_____

4. How effective was Saul's first evangelism attempt in Damascus?_____

_____

5. What happened to the Church after Saul's conversion?_____

_____

The Conversion of Cornelius

OVERVIEW

The gospel had gone out to Judea and Samaria in fulfillment of Jesus' commission in Acts 1:8, but in this lesson we see a new move of the Spirit. With clear confirmation and direction from the Lord, Peter and Cornelius, a Gentile, met together. Peter preached the gospel to Cornelius and his friends and family, and before he was finished speaking, these Gentiles received the Holy Spirit—without even getting circumcised or following the Old Testament Law. This was the beginning of the mission of the Church to the *entire* world.

SOURCE MATERIAL

- Acts 9:32-11

ACTIVITIES

1. Your Purity Standards. If your class had an encounter with a person who challenged your purity standards, reflect on the experience and answer the following questions. If that didn't happen, think of a time when you encountered someone whom you found difficult to love or who made you feel uncomfortable by being "unclean" in some way, just like Peter felt towards Cornelius. Then answer the following questions.

What was your initial reaction when you encountered the person or people?_____

_____

_____

_____

_____

_____

_____

_____

You may have pushed through it and done the right thing, but was there any desire to keep your distance or turn away? Explain._____

_____

_____

_____

_____

_____

_____

_____

Did you have a chance to make conversation with anyone? Was it difficult? How and why?_____

_____

_____

_____

_____

_____

_____

_____

Did you experience any compassion for the other person or people? What did your compassion drive you to do? Did you do it? Why or why not?_____

_____

_____

_____

_____

_____

_____

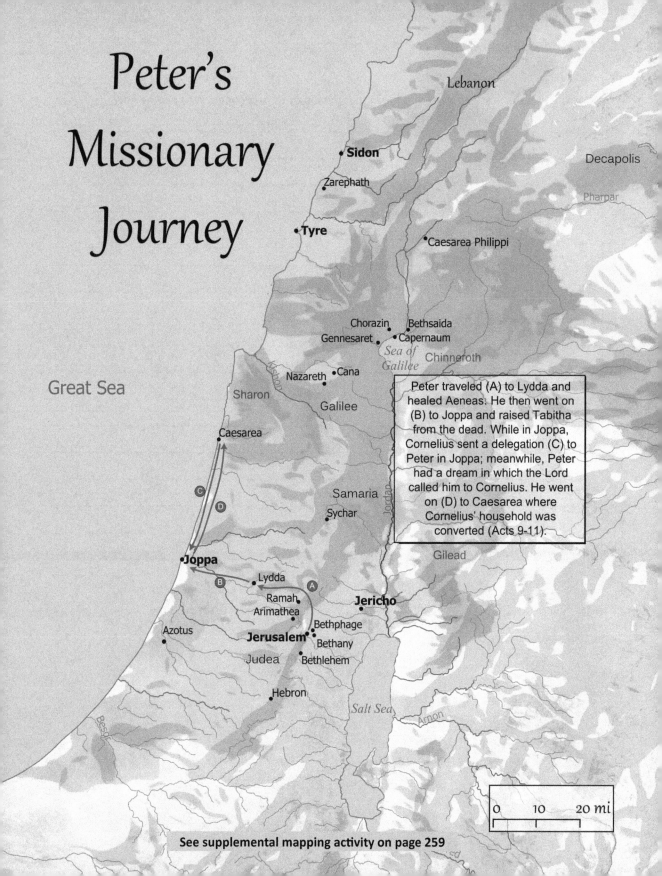

Peter's Missionary Journey

Lebanon

Decapolis

Pharpar

Sidon

Zarephath

Tyre

•Caesarea Philippi

Chorazin •Bethsaida
Gennesaret •Capernaum
Sea of Galilee   Chinneroth

Nazareth •Cana

Great Sea

Sharon

Galilee

Caesarea

Samaria

Sychar

Peter traveled (A) to Lydda and healed Aeneas. He then went on (B) to Joppa and raised Tabitha from the dead. While in Joppa, Cornelius sent a delegation (C) to Peter in Joppa; meanwhile, Peter had a dream in which the Lord called him to Cornelius. He went on (D) to Caesarea where Cornelius' household was converted (Acts 9-11).

Gilead

Joppa

Lydda
Ramah
Arimathea
Bethphage
Bethany
Bethlehem

Jericho

Jerusalem

Azotus

Judea

Hebron

Salt Sea

Arnon

0   10   20 mi

See supplemental mapping activity on page 259

Would you want to spend more time with that person or those people? Why or why not?_____

_____

_____

_____

_____

_____

What did you learn about your own standards of cleanness?_____

_____

_____

_____

_____

_____

_____

_____

_____

_____

EVALUATION

1. In what way did an understanding of Christianity as a "second story" built onto the Old Testament Law lack when it came to evangelizing? _____

_____

_____

_____

2. Where did Peter go on his first missionary journey?_____

_____

_____

3. What happened after Peter raised Tabitha from the dead?_____

_____

_____

4. What all did the Lord do to bring Peter and Cornelius together?_____

_____

_____

5. What was Cornelius' spiritual condition before he heard the gospel from Peter? _____

_____

_____

6. How was Peter's news about Cornelius received when he got back to Jerusalem?_____

_____

_____

_____

Peter's Imprisonment

OVERVIEW

Herod decided that it might be politically expedient to start persecuting the Church. He had James killed and it played well, so he arrested Peter next. Instead of killing Peter right away, Herod put him in prison so he could kill him on Passover. While in prison, Peter was miraculously delivered. The way the story is told, Peter experienced a sort of death and resurrection; then the Lord struck Herod dead.

SOURCE MATERIAL

- Acts 12

ACTIVITIES

1. Parallel Pictures. This activity is to help you see how Peter's time in prison reflected Jesus' death and resurrection. On the left side below, draw small pictures of Jesus' trial, death, and resurrection. On the right side, corresponding to each of Jesus' pictures, draw pictures of Peter's time in prison (Acts 12).

2. Lives that Reflect Jesus. Several different times in Acts we see characters whose lives reflected Jesus' life. God wants your life to be patterned after Jesus' life too. Answer the following questions to help you figure out what it might look like to reflect Jesus' life at your age and in our culture.

What is something you could do everyday that would make your life more like Jesus' life?_____

_____

_____

_____

_____

What can you do in conversations with friends that would make your life more like Jesus' life?_____

_____

_____

_____

_____

What can you do at home and with your family to make your life look more like Jesus' life?_____

_____

_____

_____

_____

What is something you can do this week to love someone sacrificially like Jesus loves us? Make this something specific and measurable. It can be something simple, but it should cost you something—whether it's time, resources, money, your image, etc._____

_____

_____

_____

_____

_____

EVALUATION

1. What was Herod's motivation in killing James and arresting Peter? _____

_____

2. What was Peter's imprisonment and release from prison a metaphor for?_____

_____

3. In what ways was Peter's experience of imprisonment like Jesus' death?_____

_____

_____

_____

4. In what ways was Peter's release from prison like Jesus' resurrection? _____

_____

_____

_____

_____

5. What happened to Herod after Peter was delivered?_____

_____

UNIT 7   **7**   **THE CHURCH EXPANDS**

Paul's First Missionary Journey

OVERVIEW

Peter's deliverance from prison and the death of Herod end the story of the growth of the Judean church in Acts, and Paul moves center stage for the Gentile expansion of Christianity. Paul and Barnabas were sent out by their home church in Antioch to bring the gospel to the Gentiles. Wherever they went, the gospel was well-received but also drew heavy fire from the enemy.

SOURCE MATERIAL

- Acts 13-14

ACTIVITIES

1. Map It. Mark and label Paul's first missionary journey on the blank map on page 220. Use the information in Acts 13-14 to construct your map.

2. Roman Culture Research. You will be assigned to a group and one of the following four topics. Your group's job is to research that aspect of Roman culture and present your findings to the class. Some possible topics for your students to research are:

- Roman religion
- Roman politics
- Roman economics
- Living conditions/standard of living for the average Roman citizen

Use the space below to record your findings, noting the ways Roman culture differed from our culture._____

_____

_____

_____

_____

(continued on next page)

_____

_____

_____

_____

_____

_____

_____

_____

_____

_____

_____

_____

_____

_____

Based on your findings, how might the gospel of Jesus Christ have been appealing to the Romans?

_____

_____

_____

_____

_____

_____

_____

EVALUATION

1. Who is the central character in the book of Acts up to chapter 13?_____

2. After Herod's death, who becomes the central character in Acts? Why?_____

_____

_____

_____

3. How did God speak to Paul and Barnabas in order to get them to go on their first missionary

journey?_____

_____

4. How were Paul and Barnabas received on their first missionary journey? _____

_____

_____

5. What did the gospel offer that was appealing to Gentile unbelievers? _____

_____

_____

6. What does the name "Paul" mean?_____

   What does "Bar-Jesus" mean?_____

   Explain the irony in these names._____

_____

7. What kind of ministry did Paul and Barnabas engage in wherever they went?_____

_____

_____

The Jerusalem Council

OVERVIEW

When Paul and Barnabas returned from their first missionary journey they were jazzed, but their celebration was quickly turned into contention when a group of Christian legalists arrived from Jerusalem. They were teaching that it was necessary to require Gentile converts to be circumcised and keep the Law of Moses in order to be saved, which obviously Paul and Barnabas had not done on their recent mission trip. The church at Antioch sent a delegation to Jerusalem to meet with the apostles and elders to get some resolution on the issue. When they arrived in Jerusalem and met with the leaders and their contenders, there was an intense disagreement. Eventually, Peter spoke and said that clearly the Lord was accepting the Gentiles without requiring them to keep the Law and so should everyone else. Paul backed Peter up with his experiences on the mission field, and James made an exegetical case from the Old Testament, proving that this was God's plan all along. The leadership sent a letter with Paul back to Antioch to settle the issue among the Gentiles.

SOURCE MATERIAL

- Acts 15:1-35
- Proverbs 18:17

ACTIVITIES

1. Act it Out. As a class, your job is to act out the Jerusalem council, especially the dispute recorded in Acts 15:4-25.

Characters

- Paul
- Barnabas
- Peter
- James
- The apostles and elders (9-15 besides Paul, Barnabas and James)
- The companions of Paul and Barnabas (at least 5)
- The Pharisees and other Judaizers (maybe 5-10)

The sequence of events is as follows:

- Paul and Barnabas arrived in Jerusalem and were greeted by the apostles and elders; they told stories about their success on the mission field and how God had been saving the Gentiles (Acts 15:4).

- Some of the believing Pharisees objected and said that it was necessary to circumcise Gentiles before they could be saved, contradicting what Paul and Barnabas had just said (Acts 15:5).

- The apostles and elders decided to have an official meeting about this issue. In the skit, this might be represented by the apostles and elders interrupting the Pharisees to say something like, "Let's not get into this argument here, let's meet on Tuesday night to discuss this all together." (Something like this is implied at the end of Acts 15:5.)

- The official meeting began and there was "much dispute" (Acts 15:6-7a). This is the part where you can come up with some of your own lines. There may have been some raised voices, but the most important thing that should come across in your skit is how these adults settled this difficult issue calmly and in a way that honored God.

- Peter spoke his part (Acts 15:7b-11).

- Paul and Barnabas explained all that they had seen the Lord do among the Gentiles (Acts 15:12).

- James made his case from Amos (Acts 15:13-21).

- The apostles and elders made an official decision and wrote a letter to send back with Paul.

2. Journal Time: What Side Am I On? This lesson provides us with a biblical way of resolving conflict. When it comes to conflict, most of us tend towards one end of the spectrum or the other. On one end of the spectrum are those who will argue just for the sake of argument and want to win at all costs, even if it means hurting someone else. On the other end of the spectrum are those who actively avoid conflict and will even sacrifice the truth in order to keep the peace. Spend some time thinking about what side of this spectrum you tend towards. Think of a specific area of conflict in your life and pray about how you can approach this conflict from a more godly perspective. Write your thoughts and prayers in the space below or in your journal._____

_____

_____

_____

_____

_____

_____

EVALUATION

1. How did the apostles and elders (Peter, Paul, James and others) know that God had accepted the Gentiles without them having to be circumcised and keep the Law?_____

_____

_____

_____

_____

2. When the apostles and elders called a meeting to deal with the question of *how* the Gentiles were saved, what was the first thing that happened? _____

_____

3. Peter was the first to silence the dispute and speak up; summarize what he said._____

_____

_____

4. In what way did Paul and Barnabas make their case that God accepted the Gentiles apart from becoming Jews?_____

_____

_____

5. What did James say to make the case from the Old Testament?_____

_____

_____

_____

6. What was the purpose of the letter that the apostles and elders wrote?_____

_____

_____

_____

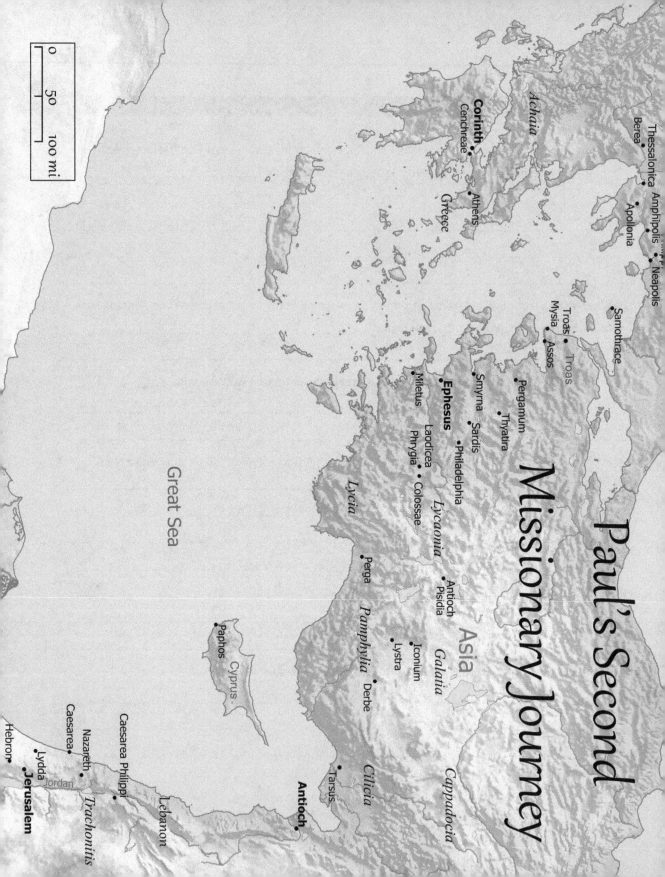

Paul's Second Missionary Journey

OVERVIEW

After returning to Antioch, Paul and Barnabas made plans to visit all the churches they had ministered in on their first missionary journey. But they strongly disagreed on whether or not to take John Mark with them. Their disagreement was so strong that they finally went in different directions. Their split ended up working out for good, allowing Barnabas to visit the churches from their previous trip and freeing Paul to cover new ground where he shared the gospel, cast out demons and saw the kingdom of God break Roman society and bring new life to the Gentiles.

SOURCE MATERIAL

- Acts 15:36-18:22

ACTIVITIES

1. Journal Time: Bless the Broken. According to Romans 12:14, we are to bless those who persecute us. By blessing others in the name of Jesus, we can be a part of rebuilding a resurrected Christianity in our world.

What are some specific and practical things you can do or say to bless others?_____

_____

_____

How can you act on these ideas this week?_____

_____

_____

After blessing someone, write about your experience below. _____

_____

_____

_____

_____

2. Think it Through. Paul and Barnabas had a major disagreement over whether or not they should bring John Mark on their second missionary journey. The disagreement was so acute that they ended up going separate ways. This turned out to be a good thing for the furtherance of the gospel as Barnabas was able to go back and encourage those they had visited on their first missionary journey, leaving Paul free to go on to Macedonia and preach the gospel in new cities. Nevertheless, it seems odd to us that men like Paul and Barnabas would have such a sharp disagreement. The Bible doesn't give us all the details of the disagreement, but we have enough to get an idea of what might have happened. Consider Acts 13:13, 15:36-41 and Colossians 4:10 and answer the questions below.

Why was Paul convinced that it was a bad idea to take John Mark with them?_____

_____

What arguments do you think Paul used with Barnabas?_____

_____

_____

Why do you think Barnabas was determined to take John Mark with them?_____

_____

What do their differences tell you about their personalities?_____

_____

What do you think was the right thing to do?_____

_____

Is it okay for Christians to disagree on something like this? Were Paul and Barnabas sinning by disagreeing and going different directions?_____

_____

How will seeing this disagreement teach you to think about disagreements you will inevitably see between godly people you respect in the future?_____

_____

3. Map it. Mark and label Paul's second missionary journey on the blank map on page 228. Use the information in Acts 15:36-18:22 to construct your map.

EVALUATION

1. What did Paul and Barnabas want to accomplish on their second missionary journey? _____

_____

_____

_____

2. Paul and Barnabas disagreed on whether to take John Mark and ended up going separate ways—
was this a good or a bad thing?_____

_____

_____

3. Everywhere Paul went, the gospel caused a violent reaction from pagans. Why was this?_____

_____

_____

_____

4. Name one way the gospel threatened pagan society._____

_____

Paul's Third Missionary Journey

OVERVIEW

After a stop in Jerusalem and some time in his home base, Antioch, Paul set out on his third missionary journey in order to encourage the disciples. He passed through Galatia and then came to Ephesus where he stayed for two years, training disciples in the school of Tyrannus. At the end of his time in Ephesus a great riot broke out in the city against the Christians because Christianity was (rightly) perceived as a threat to the idol-making business. Following the turmoil in Ephesus, Paul went through Macedonia and Greece and then set his face toward Jerusalem.

SOURCE MATERIAL

- Acts 18:23-21:16

ACTIVITIES

1. Doubling Disciples. The gospel doesn't transform society by high-powered evangelists and pastors spreading the gospel in large venues. The gospel transforms the world when disciples make disciples in order to disciple others. That is not to say that there isn't a time and place for spreading the gospel in large group settings. The book of Acts gives numerous examples of Paul sharing the gospel in the synagogues and public places in front of large crowds. However, the majority of Paul's (and Jesus') time was spent discipling others. After your teacher leads you in an activity to help you see how powerful discipleship can be, write your reflections below._____

_____

_____

_____

_____

_____

_____

2. Journal Time: Discipleship. As evidenced by Paul's and Jesus' lives, discipleship is central to the Christian faith. It is not only an excellent means of spreading the good news, it also helps Christians grow in their faith and learn from one another. Take some time to reflect on your experience with discipleship and how you can more effectively be discipled and disciple others; then answer the questions below.

What is your experience with being discipled? _____

_____

_____

_____

_____

_____

_____

Are you currently being discipled? _____

If not, how can you put yourself in a position to be discipled? _____

_____

_____

_____

_____

_____

_____

Who are some people you could ask to disciple you?_____

_____

_____

_____

_____

(continued on next page)

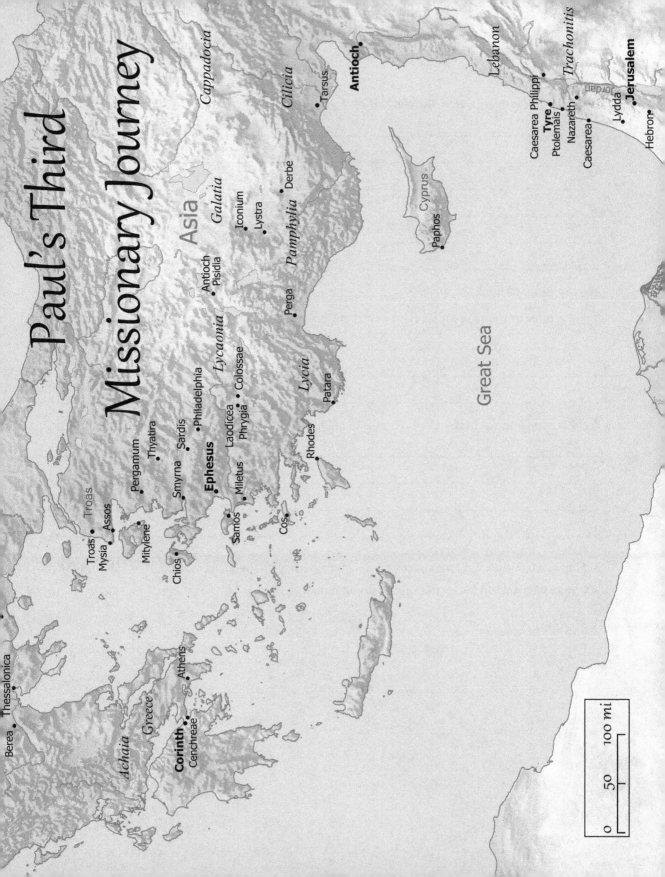

Paul's Third
Missionary Journey

Antioch

Tarsus

Cilicia

Cappadocia

Asia

Galatia

Iconium

Lystra

Derbe

Antioch
Pisidia

Pamphylia

Perga

Lycaonia

Colossae

Phrygia

Philadelphia

Laodicea

Thyatira

Sardis

Pergamum

Smyrna

Ephesus

Miletus

Samos

Cos

Rhodes

Lycia

Patara

Troas

Mysia Assos

Mitylene

Chios

Greece

Thessalonica

Berea

Athens

Corinth

Cenchreae

Achaia

Cyprus

Paphos

Lebanon

Caesarea Philippi

Tyre
Ptolemais

Nazareth

Caesarea

Jordan

Trachonitis

Jerusalem

Lydda

Hebron

Great Sea

100 mi

50

0

What is your experience with discipling others? _____

_____

_____

_____

_____

_____

_____

Are you currently discipling anyone? _____

If not, is there anyone in your life right now that God may be leading you to disciple? _____

_____

_____

_____

What are some concrete steps you can take to disciple that person?_____

_____

_____

_____

_____

3. Map It. Mark and label Paul's second missionary journey on the blank map on page 235. Use the information in Acts 18:23-21:16 to construct your map.

EVALUATION

1. What did Paul do for two years while in Ephesus on his third missionary journey? _____

_____

_____

2. What happened when the sons of Sceva attempted to use Jesus' name as an incantation to cast out demons?_____

_____

_____

_____

_____

3. What caused the riot in Ephesus during Paul's third missionary journey?_____

_____

_____

4. What is one way Paul was like Jesus?_____

_____

_____

_____

_____

5. What was the most significant thing Paul did on these missionary journeys?_____

_____

OVERVIEW

Paul was the new Jesus. He was arrested in Jerusalem and tried before the Sanhedrin, the local Roman authorities and Herod. But he didn't die in Jerusalem. He was taken to Rome where he was put under house arrest. The book of Acts never tells us the end of Paul's story—to this day, the Church continues the story from where he left off.

SOURCE MATERIAL

- Acts 21:17-28:30

ACTIVITIES

1. Finish the Story. Acts is an unfinished story. Paul went to Rome and was under house arrest, but ministered the gospel to many visitors. We never hear about what happened to Paul in Rome. Of course, from Church history we know he was martyred, but Acts ends mid-story for a purpose. It is our story, and it's not finished yet. Read through Matthew 28:18-20 and Acts 1:8 and answer the questions below. Be prepared to discuss your answers in class.

Name five things that Paul did throughout his ministry to fulfill Jesus' commissions from Matthew 28:18-20 and Acts 1:8._____

_____

_____

_____

_____

_____

_____

_____

How many of those things are you presently doing? _____

_____

_____

_____

How many are you not presently doing that you are capable of doing?_____

_____

_____

_____

_____

_____

What would it take to start doing them?_____

_____

_____

_____

Which things are you not presently able to do? Why not?_____

_____

_____

_____

_____

Write a prayer asking God to guide you in your efforts to reach your neighbors. _____

_____

_____

_____

_____

_____

_____

2. Journal Time: Your Story. Paul used the story of his conversion over and over again when he had the chance to speak to unbelievers in a public forum. He did this because it demonstrated that Jesus was alive—Paul had actually met Jesus and been set free.

Do you have a story of meeting Jesus? We are not simply asking about when you got saved. Maybe that's your story of meeting Jesus, but many people don't really meet Him in a deep and personal way until they are going through a hard time and He steps in to speak to them. If you do have a story, write the short version of it below as though you are telling it to an unbeliever._____

_____

_____

_____

_____

_____

_____

_____

_____

_____

_____

_____

If you haven't met Jesus, write a short prayer asking Him to show Himself to you in an unmistakable and deeply personal way._____

_____

_____

_____

3. Map It. Mark and label Paul's arrest and journey to Rome on the blank map on page 244. Use the information in Acts 18:23-21:16 to construct your map.

EVALUATION

1. What was the "official" reason that Paul was arrested in Jerusalem? _____

_____

_____

2. What did Paul seek to do as soon as he was arrested? _____

_____

_____

3. How did Paul go about preaching the gospel? _____

_____

4. Why do you think Paul used his own story to share the gospel?_____

_____

_____

_____

5. Jesus was tried before three different authorities: the Sanhedrin, the Roman authorities and Herod. How many of these same authorities was Paul tried before? _____

6. In what way did Paul's story differ from Jesus'? _____

_____

_____

7. What compelled the Roman military to take Paul to Caesarea?_____

_____

9. What did Paul do to get himself transferred to Rome?_____

_____

   How does Acts end? _____

_____

10. Why do you think Acts ends this way?_____

_____

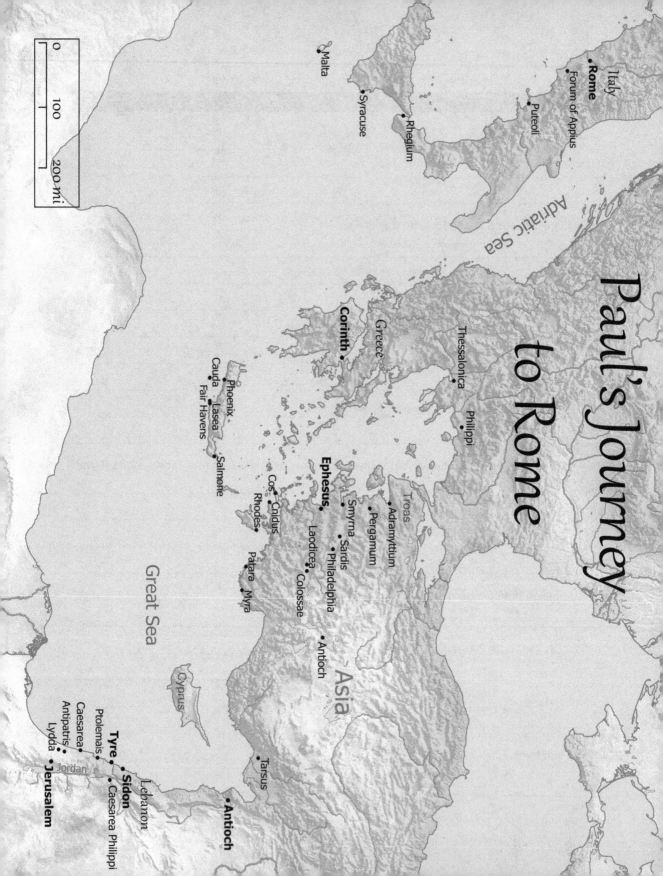

Paul's Journey to Rome

Italy

• Rome
Forum of Appius
• Puteoli

Adriatic Sea

• Malta

• Syracuse

• Rhegium

Great Sea

Scale:
0
100
200 mi

Corinth •

Greece

Thessalonica •

Philippi •

Cauda •
Phoenix •
Lasea •
Fair Havens

Salmone •

Cos •
Rhodes •
Cnidus •

Ephesus •

Smyrna •
Pergamum •

Troas •
Adramyttium •

Sardis •
Philadelphia •
Laodicea •
Colossae •

Patara •
Myra •

Antioch •

Asia

Cyprus

Tarsus •

Tyre •
Sidon •
Caesarea Philippi •

Ptolemais •
Caesarea •
Antipatris •
Lydda •
Jordan

Jerusalem •

Lebanon

Antioch •

END OF YEAR ACTIVITIES

1. **Highs and Lows.** The Story of God's people is filled with highs and lows. As a class or in groups, draw a graph of the New Testament Story. Begin with a horizontal timeline of the Story from Jesus' birth to Paul's house arrest in Rome. Then add a vertical axis, charting the lowest, most discouraging points in the Story at the bottom and the most blessed high points at the very top. If it helps, you can subdivide this activity into two sections (the life of Jesus and the early Church).

2. **The Spread of the Gospel.** On a large map of the world of the New Testament, chart the geographical spread of the gospel, starting with Pentecost and working through the dispersions and missionary journeys of the New Testament. When you get done with the New Testament, find your *location* on the map. How'd that happen?

3. **Your Gospel Genealogy.** Map their own gospel genealogy back as far as you can. Who is primarily responsible for telling you about Jesus? Who told that person? See if you can trace your gospel genealogy farther than any of your classmates. Furthermore, though we don't know the names, all of these genealogies go back to someone who was there at Pentecost, and from there to Jesus. Jesus told someone about Himself, and that person told someone else, and so on for 2,000 years, down to the names we still remember. Join this history and become part of someone else's gospel genealogy.

4. **Timeline.** On the paper your teacher has posted around the classroom, make an illustrated timeline of the New Testament Story.

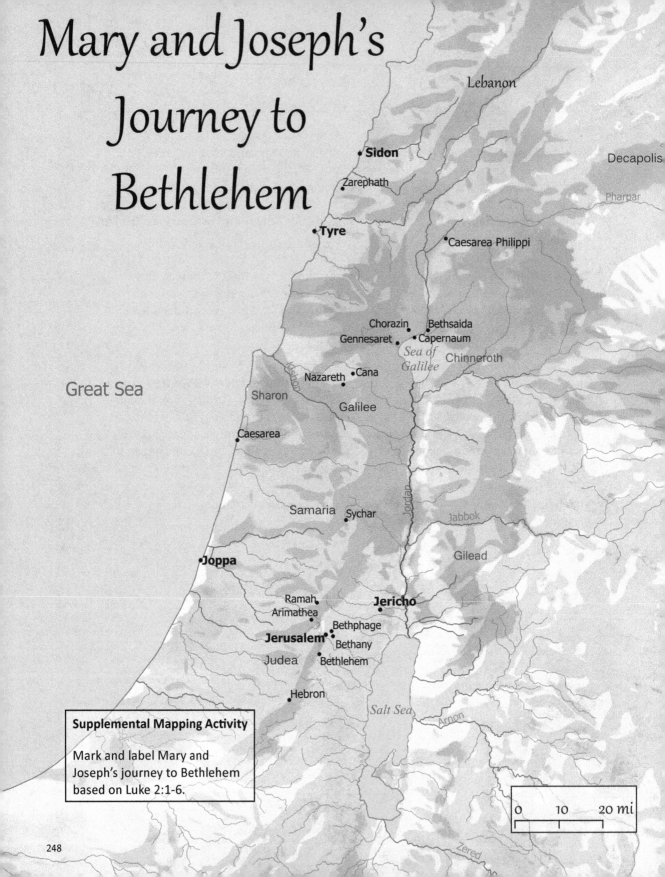

Mary and Joseph's Journey to Bethlehem

Lebanon

Decapolis

Sidon

Zarephath

Pharpar

Tyre

• Caesarea Philippi

Chorazin   Bethsaida

Gennesaret   • Capernaum

Sea of Galilee

Chinneroth

Nazareth   • Cana

Great Sea

Sharon

Galilee

Kishon

Caesarea

Samaria   Sychar

Jordan

Jabbok

Gilead

Joppa

Ramah
Arimathea

Jericho

Bethphage

Jerusalem

Bethany

Judea   Bethlehem

Hebron

Salt Sea

Arnon

Supplemental Mapping Activity

Mark and label Mary and
Joseph's journey to Bethlehem
based on Luke 2:1-6.

0   10   20 mi

Zered

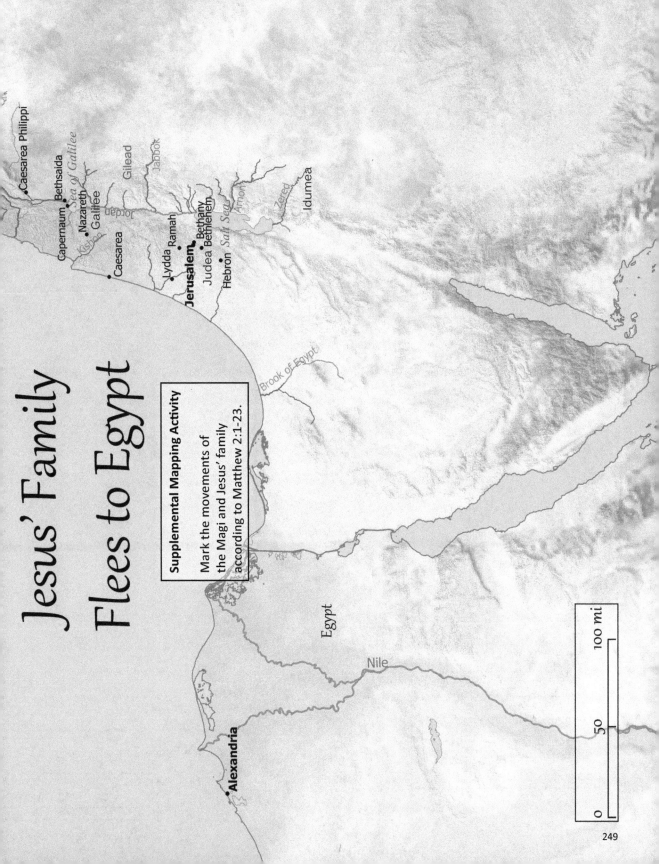

Jesus' Family
Flees to Egypt

Supplemental Mapping Activity

Mark the movements of
the Magi and Jesus' family
according to Matthew 2:1-23.

Caesarea Philippi

Bethsaida

Capernaum

Sea of Galilee

Nazareth

Galilee

Gilead

Jabbok

Jordan

Kishon

Caesarea

Lydda

Ramah

Bethany

Bethlehem

Jerusalem

Judea

Hebron

Salt Sea

Arnon

Zered

Idumea

Brook of Egypt

Egypt

Nile

Alexandria

0	50	100 mi

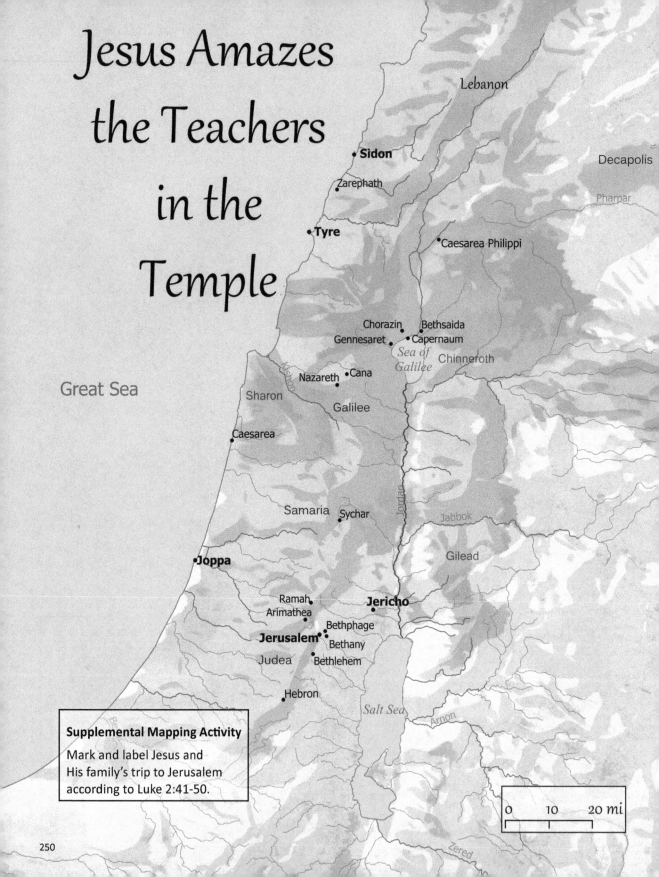

Jesus Amazes the Teachers in the Temple

Lebanon

Decapolis

Sidon

Zarephath

Pharpar

Tyre

Caesarea Philippi

Chorazin

Bethsaida

Gennesaret

Capernaum

Sea of Galilee

Chinneroth

Nazareth

Cana

Galilee

Great Sea

Sharon

Caesarea

Samaria

Sychar

Jordan

Jabbok

Gilead

Joppa

Ramah

Arimathea

Jericho

Bethphage

Jerusalem

Bethany

Judea

Bethlehem

Hebron

Salt Sea

Arnon

Zered

Supplemental Mapping Activity

Mark and label Jesus and His family's trip to Jerusalem according to Luke 2:41-50.

| 0 | 10 | 20 mi |

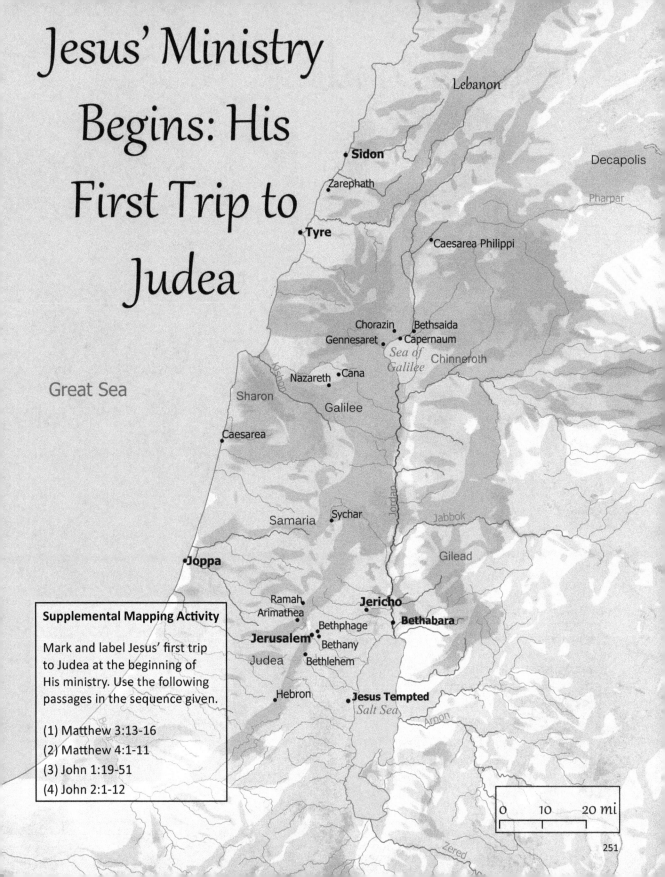

Jesus' Ministry Begins: His First Trip to Judea

Lebanon

Decapolis

• **Sidon**

Zarephath

Pharpar

• **Tyre**

• Caesarea Philippi

Chorazin • Bethsaida

Gennesaret • • Capernaum

Sea of Galilee

Chinneroth

Nazareth • • Cana

Galilee

Great Sea

Sharon

Kishon

• Caesarea

Samaria • Sychar

Jordan

Jabbok

Gilead

• **Joppa**

Ramah •

Arimathea •

• **Jericho**

Bethphage •

• **Bethabara**

Jerusalem •

• Bethany

Judea

• Bethlehem

Hebron •

• **Jesus Tempted**

Salt Sea

Arnon

Zered

Supplemental Mapping Activity

Mark and label Jesus' first trip to Judea at the beginning of His ministry. Use the following passages in the sequence given.

(1) Matthew 3:13-16
(2) Matthew 4:1-11
(3) John 1:19-51
(4) John 2:1-12

0   10   20 mi

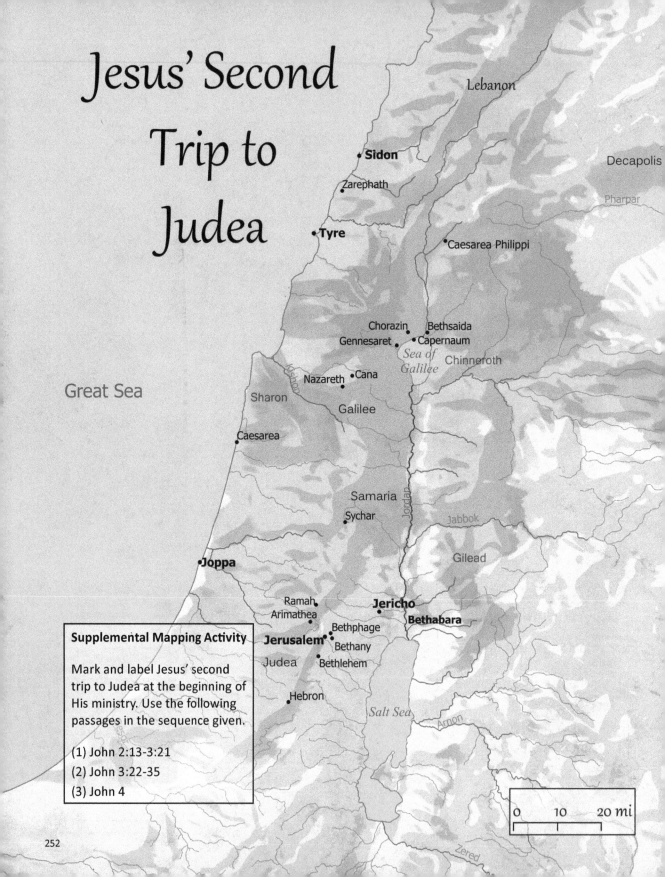

Jesus' Second Trip to Judea

Lebanon

Decapolis

Pharpar

Sidon

Zarephath

Tyre

Caesarea Philippi

Great Sea

Chorazin   Bethsaida
Gennesaret   • Capernaum
                    Sea of
                    Galilee   Chinneroth

Nazareth • Cana

Sharon   Galilee

Caesarea

Samaria

Sychar

Jordan   Jabbok

Gilead

Joppa

Ramah
Arimathea   **Jericho**
        Bethphage   **Bethabara**

Jerusalem   Bethany

Judea   Bethlehem

Hebron

Salt Sea

Arnon

Supplemental Mapping Activity

Mark and label Jesus' second
trip to Judea at the beginning of
His ministry. Use the following
passages in the sequence given.

(1) John 2:13-3:21
(2) John 3:22-35
(3) John 4

0   10   20 mi

Zered

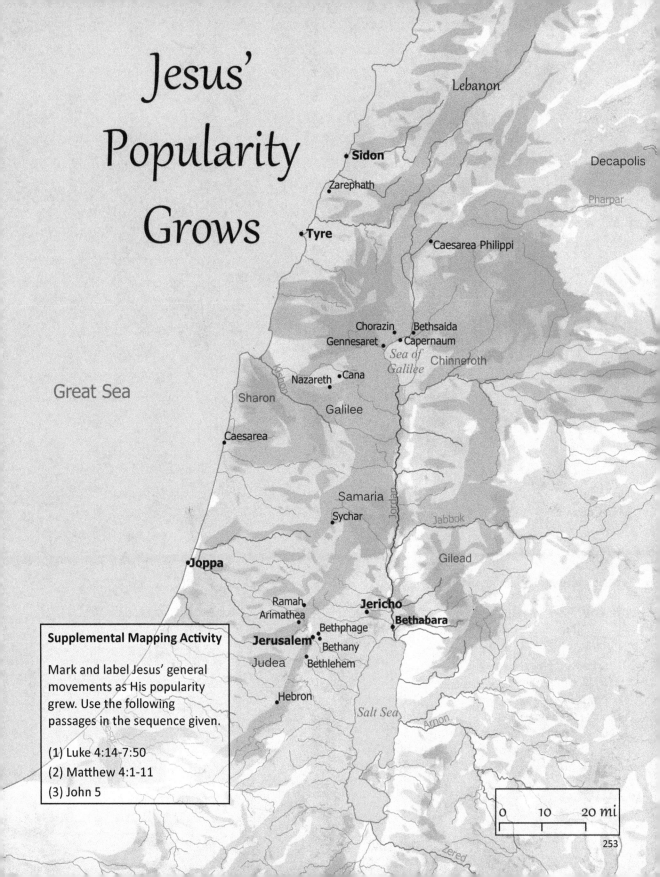

Jesus' Popularity Grows

Lebanon

Sidon

Zarephath

Tyre

Decapolis

Pharpar

Caesarea Philippi

Great Sea

Chorazin • Bethsaida
Gennesaret • Capernaum

Sea of Galilee

Chinneroth

Nazareth • Cana

Galilee

Sharon

Caesarea

Samaria

Sychar

Jordan

Jabbok

Gilead

Joppa

Ramah
Arimathea

Bethphage

Jericho

Bethabara

Jerusalem

Bethany

Judea

Bethlehem

Hebron

Salt Sea

Arnon

Zered

Supplemental Mapping Activity

Mark and label Jesus' general
movements as His popularity
grew. Use the following
passages in the sequence given.

(1) Luke 4:14-7:50

(2) Matthew 4:1-11

(3) John 5

0   10   20 mi

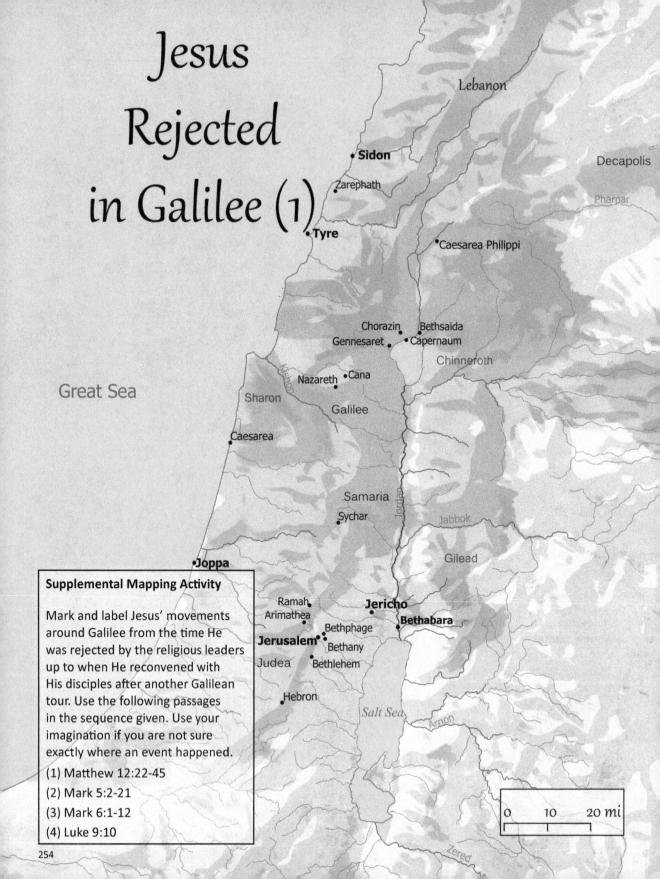

Jesus Rejected in Galilee (1)

Lebanon

Decapolis

Sidon

Zarephath

Pharpar

Tyre

Caesarea Philippi

Chorazin • Bethsaida
Gennesaret • Capernaum

Chinneroth

Nazareth • Cana

Great Sea

Sharon

Galilee

Caesarea

Samaria

Jordan

Sychar

Jabbok

Gilead

Joppa

Supplemental Mapping Activity

Mark and label Jesus' movements around Galilee from the time He was rejected by the religious leaders up to when He reconvened with His disciples after another Galilean tour. Use the following passages in the sequence given. Use your imagination if you are not sure exactly where an event happened.

(1) Matthew 12:22-45

(2) Mark 5:2-21

(3) Mark 6:1-12

(4) Luke 9:10

Ramah
Arimathea

Jericho

Bethphage

Bethabara

Jerusalem •
Bethany

Judea
Bethlehem

Hebron

Salt Sea

Arnon

0   10   20 mi

Zered

Jesus Rejected in Galilee (2)

Tyre — Jesus delivered the Syrophoenician woman's daughter.

Caesarea Philippi.

Chorazin

Bethsaida

Jesus went up on a mountain to pray by Himself.

Capernaum.

Gennesaret.

Feeding of 5,000

Magdala.

Tiberias.

Chinneroth

Sea of Galilee

Feeding of 4,000

Supplemental Mapping Activity

Mark and label Jesus' general movements around Galilee from when He crossed the Sea to feed the 5,000 up to the feeding of the 4,000. Use the following passages in the sequence given. Some locations are marked on the map; use your imagination if you are not sure exactly where an event happened.

(1) Luke 9:10
(2) Matt 14:13
(3) Matt 14:22-33
(4) John 6:22-71
(5) Matt 14:34-46
(6) Mark 7:31-8:13

0   5   10 mi

Jesus Rejected in Galilee (3)

Tyre

Caesarea Philippi

Jesus' ministry in the region of Caesarea Philippi

Transfiguration

Chorazin

Bethsaida

Capernaum

Gennesaret

Magdala

Tiberias

Sea of Galilee

Chinneroth

Feeding of 4,000

Supplemental Mapping Activity

Mark and label Jesus' general movements around Galilee from the feeding of the 4,000 up to His return to Galilee after the transfiguration. Use the following passages in the sequence given. Some locations are marked on the map, use your imagination if you are not sure exactly where an event happened.

(1) Mark 7:31-8:13

(2) Matt 15:38

(3) Matt 16:1-12

(4) Matt 16:13, Mark 8:22

(5) Matt 17:1-12

| 0 | 5 | 10 mi |

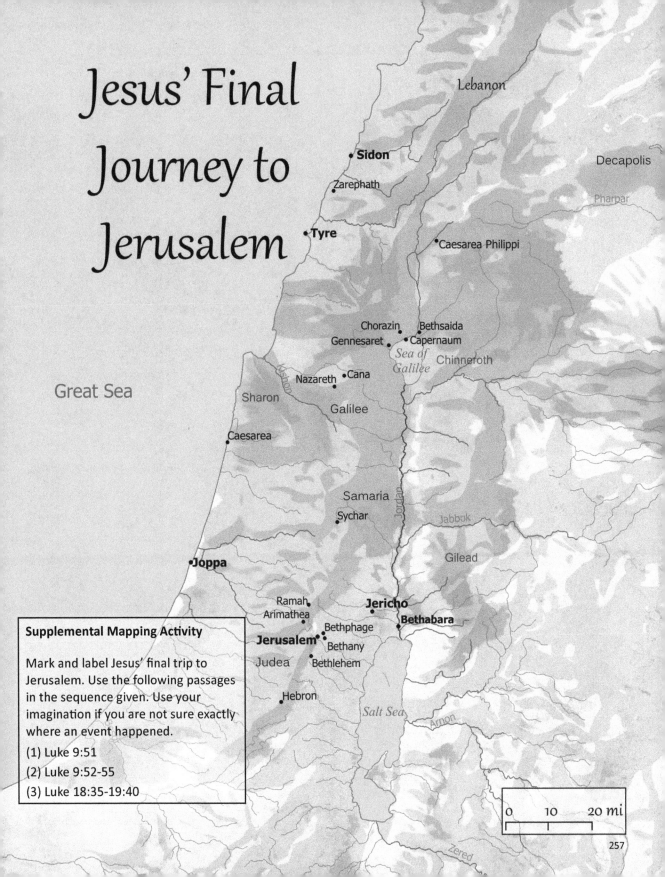

Jesus' Final Journey to Jerusalem

Lebanon

Sidon

Decapolis

Zarephath

Pharpar

Tyre

Caesarea Philippi

Chorazin Bethsaida

Gennesaret Capernaum

Sea of Galilee Chinneroth

Nazareth Cana

Great Sea

Sharon

Galilee

Caesarea

Samaria

Jordan

Sychar

Jabbok

Gilead

Joppa

Ramah Jericho
Arimathea Bethphage **Bethabara**
Jerusalem Bethany
Judea Bethlehem

Hebron

Salt Sea

Arnon

Supplemental Mapping Activity

Mark and label Jesus' final trip to Jerusalem. Use the following passages in the sequence given. Use your imagination if you are not sure exactly where an event happened.

(1) Luke 9:51

(2) Luke 9:52-55

(3) Luke 18:35-19:40

0   10   20 mi

Zered

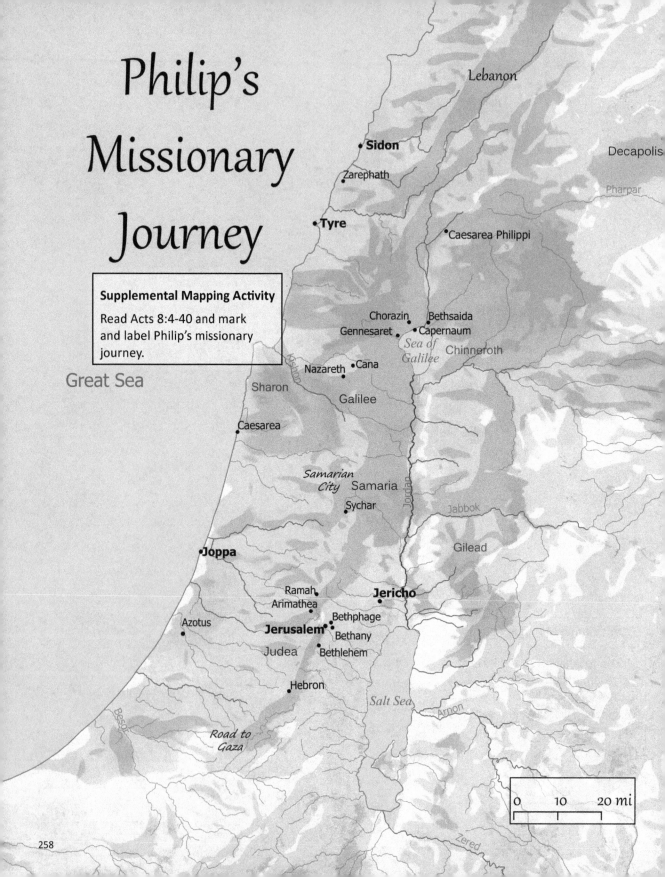

Philip's Missionary Journey

Supplemental Mapping Activity

Read Acts 8:4-40 and mark and label Philip's missionary journey.

Lebanon

Decapolis

Pharpar

Sidon

Zarephath

Tyre

Caesarea Philippi

Chorazin   Bethsaida

Gennesaret   Capernaum

Sea of Galilee   Chinneroth

Nazareth   •Cana

Galilee

Great Sea

Sharon

Caesarea

Samarian City   Samaria

Sychar

Jordan

Jabbok

Gilead

Joppa

Ramah   **Jericho**

Arimathea

Bethphage

Azotus   **Jerusalem**   Bethany

Judea   Bethlehem

Hebron

Salt Sea

Arnon

Besor

Road to Gaza

Zered

0   10   20 mi

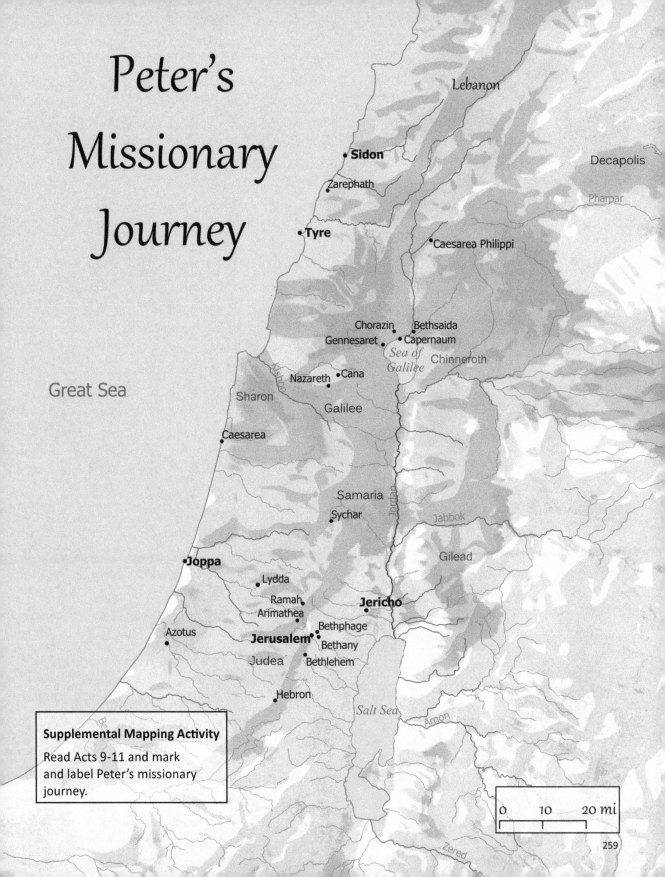

Peter's Missionary Journey

Lebanon

Decapolis

Pharpar

Sidon

Zarephath

Tyre

Caesarea Philippi

Chorazin   Bethsaida

Gennesaret   Capernaum

Sea of Galilee

Chinneroth

Nazareth   Cana

Galilee

Great Sea

Sharon

Caesarea

Samaria

Sychar

Jordan

Jabbok

Gilead

Joppa

Lydda

Ramah

Arimathea

Jericho

Bethphage

Azotus

Jerusalem

Bethany

Judea   Bethlehem

Hebron

Salt Sea

Arnon

Supplemental Mapping Activity

Read Acts 9-11 and mark and label Peter's missionary journey.

0   10   20 mi

Zered